WILLIAMS-SONOMA

STEAK & CHOP

RECIPES AND TEXT
DENIS KELLY

GENERAL EDITOR
CHUCK WILLIAMS

PHOTOGRAPHS
MAREN CARUSO

SIMON & SCHUSTER • **SOURCE**

NEW YORK • LONDON • TORONTO • SYDNEY • SINGAPORE

CONTENTS

THE CLASSICS

QUICK WEEKNIGHT DISHES

ELEGANT OCCASIONS

SUMMER GRILLING

WINTER FARE

HOLIDAY FEASTS

INTRODUCTION

Enjoying a tender filet mignon or savory pork chop is one of life's simple pleasures, whether the meat is slow-roasted with an herb rub, grilled over hot coals, or quickly sautéed and served with an easy pan sauce. The wide variety of steak and chop recipes in these pages includes something for every occasion, from wonderful dishes for entertaining to fresh ideas for the summer grill, along with a selection of easy weeknight suppers. An entire chapter of recipes for larger cuts of meat that are carved into chops—such as crown roast of pork—will certainly come in handy for the holidays or large parties throughout the year.

Preparing steaks or chops often takes just minutes, but you can bring out the best in each cut of meat with the right cooking method and a few specific skills, such as knowing how to test for doneness or carve a large roast. For advice, turn to the informative basics section at the back of the book, where you will find what you need to know. I am confident that you will come back to the satisfying recipes in this book time and time again.

Chuck Williams

THE CLASSICS

When you think of steaks and chops, certain classic preparations come immediately to mind. Favorites such as succulent filets mignons with a rich Cognac-cream sauce, spicy steak au poivre, and tender lamb chops paired with mint are just a few recipes that make the perfect centerpiece for any occasion.

FILETS MIGNONS WITH COGNAC-CREAM SAUCE
10

STEAK AU POIVRE WITH RED WINE PAN SAUCE
13

GRILLED RIB STEAKS WITH ASPARAGUS
14

STUFFED PORK CHOPS WITH SHERRY GRAVY
17

GRILLED LAMB CHOPS WITH
MINT-MASCARPONE PESTO
18

GRILLED VEAL CHOPS WITH TARRAGON
21

CHATEAUBRIAND WITH BÉARNAISE SAUCE
22

T-BONE STEAKS WITH
ROQUEFORT ROASTED TOMATOES
24

FILETS MIGNONS WITH COGNAC-CREAM SAUCE

TESTING DONENESS

The easiest way to check meat or poultry for doneness is by inserting an instant-read thermometer into the thickest part of the meat away from the bone. You can also cut into the meat to check how pink the interior is, although this method has the disadvantage of possibly marring a pristine cut of meat.

Another trick for steaks or chops is to prod the top with your finger, then poke the muscle at the base of your thumb when you make a fist. They'll feel similar when the meat is medium-rare. For more details on testing doneness, see page 109.

To make the rub, in a small bowl, mix together the paprika, garlic powder, mustard, rosemary, salt, and black pepper. Sprinkle the rub all over the meat, reserving 1 tablespoon. Let the steaks stand at room temperature for at least 15 minutes or up to 1 hour, or cover and refrigerate overnight. Bring to room temperature, if necessary, before cooking.

In a large, heavy frying pan over medium-high heat, heat the olive oil. Add the steaks and cook to the desired doneness, turning once, 3–5 minutes on each side. Test for doneness using an instant-read thermometer or by cutting into the meat. Remove the steaks from the heat when they are red at the center for rare (120°F/49°C) or deep pink at the center for medium-rare (130°F/54°C). Transfer the steaks to a platter and let rest, tented loosely with aluminum foil, while you make the pan sauce.

To make the sauce, in the same frying pan over medium heat, melt the butter. Add the shallot and parsley and sauté until the shallot is softened, 2–3 minutes. Remove the pan from the heat and add the Cognac. Briefly return to the heat to warm; then remove from the heat again to ignite the Cognac using a long kitchen match, making sure the overhead fan is off and averting your eyes. Keep a lid handy in case the flame should flare up. When the flame has burned out, return the pan to high heat and whisk in the mustard, tomato paste, reserved 1 tablespoon rub, and beef stock. Cook, whisking often, to reduce the sauce by half, 4–5 minutes. Remove the pan from the heat and whisk in the cream and cayenne to taste. Add any accumulated juices from the steaks. Season to taste with salt and black pepper.

To serve, spoon a generous amount of sauce over the steaks and serve at once. Pass any extra sauce at the table.

MAKES 4 SERVINGS

FOR THE RUB:

1 tablespoon *each* paprika, garlic powder, dry mustard, and dried rosemary

1½ teaspoons salt

1 teaspoon freshly ground black pepper

4 filet mignon steaks, 1½ inches (4 cm) thick

1 tablespoon olive oil

FOR THE SAUCE:

1 tablespoon unsalted butter

1 shallot, minced

2 tablespoons minced fresh flat-leaf (Italian) parsley

2 tablespoons Cognac

1 tablespoon Dijon mustard

2 tablespoons tomato paste

1 cup (8 fl oz/250 ml) beef stock (page 110)

½ cup (4 fl oz/125 ml) heavy (double) cream

Cayenne pepper

Salt and freshly ground black pepper

STEAK AU POIVRE WITH RED WINE PAN SAUCE

4 boneless beef sirloin
steaks, at least 1 inch
(2.5 cm) thick, trimmed
of excess fat

Salt

1 tablespoon cracked
black peppercorns

1 tablespoon olive oil

FOR THE PAN SAUCE:

1 tablespoon unsalted
butter

½ red onion, finely
chopped

1 clove garlic, minced

½ cup (4 fl oz/125 ml)
dry red wine

1 cup (8 fl oz/250 ml)
beef stock (page 110)
or prepared broth, plus
more if needed

1 tablespoon tomato paste

1 tablespoon cornstarch
(cornflour) combined with
2 tablespoons water

2 tablespoons chopped
fresh flat-leaf (Italian)
parsley

Salt and freshly ground
pepper

Slash the edges of the steaks in 1 or 2 places to prevent curling. Sprinkle all sides generously with salt and cracked black pepper, pressing the pepper into the surface of the meat. Let the steaks stand at room temperature for at least 15 minutes and up to 1 hour before cooking.

In a large, heavy frying pan over medium-high heat, heat the olive oil. Add the steaks and cook to the desired doneness, turning once, 3–5 minutes on each side. Test for doneness using an instant-read thermometer or by cutting into the meat. Remove the steaks from the heat when they are red at the center for rare (120°F/49°C) or deep pink at the center for medium-rare (130°F/54°C). Transfer to a platter and let rest, tented loosely with aluminum foil, while you make the pan sauce.

To make the pan sauce, in the same frying pan over medium-high heat, melt the butter. Add the onion and garlic and sauté until the onion is softened, 3–5 minutes. Add the wine and stock and boil until reduced by half, 4–5 minutes. Reduce the heat to medium, whisk in the tomato paste and cornstarch mixture, and simmer, whisking occasionally, until slightly thickened, 3–5 minutes. Add more stock if the sauce seems too thick. Stir in the parsley and season to taste with salt and pepper.

To serve, spoon a generous amount of sauce over the steaks and serve at once. Pass any extra sauce at the table.

MAKES 4 SERVINGS

MAKING PAN SAUCES

To make a sauce in the pan you've just used to cook meat, first add a little olive oil and sauté minced garlic or shallot, then pour in wine, stock, or another liquid to deglaze the pan, scraping up any browned bits from the bottom. Next stir in seasonings such as herbs, mustard, tomato paste, Worcestershire sauce, or soy sauce. Thicken the sauce by reducing it over high heat or by stirring in a little cornstarch mixed with water and cooking for a few minutes longer. For a richer sauce, stir in 2 tablespoons heavy (double) cream or chilled unsalted butter at the end.

GRILLED RIB STEAKS WITH ASPARAGUS

RUBS AND PASTES

Mixtures of fresh or dried herbs, garlic, salt, and pepper add wonderful flavor when rubbed on chops, steaks, and roasts before cooking. You can also make a wet rub or paste by combining the same ingredients with olive oil and/or a bit of lemon juice. In this recipe, you could substitute tarragon, oregano, or other herbs for the thyme. Herb rubs and pastes often include chiles (fresh or dried), mustard, soy sauce, or chopped fresh ginger. Once you've rubbed the meat with your rub or paste, let it sit for at least 15 minutes or up to 1 hour before cooking.

To make the herb rub, in a small bowl, mix together the paprika, garlic powder, thyme, salt, and pepper. Slash the edges of the steaks in 2 or 3 places to prevent curling. Rub the mixture all over the meat and let stand at room temperature for at least 15 minutes or up to 1 hour, or cover and refrigerate overnight. Bring to room temperature, if necessary, before grilling.

Prepare a charcoal or gas grill for direct grilling over medium-high heat (page 106). Grill the steaks to the desired doneness, turning once, 3–5 minutes on each side. (Move them to a cooler area of the grill if flare-ups occur.) Test for doneness using an instant-read thermometer or by cutting into the meat. Remove the steaks from the heat when they are red at the center for rare (120°F/49°C) or deep pink at the center for medium-rare (130°F/54°C). Transfer the steaks to a platter and let rest for 5 minutes, tented loosely with aluminum foil, before serving.

Meanwhile, trim or snap off the tough ends of the asparagus spears. In a small bowl, whisk together the olive oil, soy sauce, mustard, lemon juice, and hot chile oil to taste. Brush the asparagus lightly with the soy sauce mixture and grill them over medium-high heat, turning often and brushing occasionally with additional soy sauce mixture, until crisp-tender, 4–5 minutes. Transfer to a platter and pour any leftover soy sauce mixture on top.

Serve each diner a steak with asparagus on the side and with a serving of scalloped potatoes, if you wish.

MAKES 4 SERVINGS

FOR THE HERB RUB:

1 tablespoon paprika

1 tablespoon garlic powder

2 tablespoons chopped fresh thyme or 1 tablespoon dried

2 teaspoons salt

1 teaspoon freshly ground pepper

4 rib steaks, at least 1½ inches (4 cm) thick, trimmed of excess fat

1 lb (500 g) thick asparagus spears

2 tablespoons olive oil

1 tablespoon soy sauce

1 tablespoon Dijon mustard

1 tablespoon fresh lemon juice

1 or 2 dashes of Asian hot chile oil

Scalloped potatoes for serving (page 110) (optional)

STUFFED PORK CHOPS WITH SHERRY GRAVY

4 bone-in pork chops,
2 inches (5 cm) thick,
trimmed of excess fat

Salt and freshly ground
pepper

4 tablespoons (2 fl oz/
60 ml) olive oil

1 yellow onion, finely
chopped

2 cloves garlic, finely
chopped

1 stalk celery, finely
chopped

1 teaspoon dried sage

1 cup (4 oz/125 g) dried
bread crumbs

2 tablespoons chopped
fresh flat-leaf (Italian)
parsley

1 tablespoon sherry,
plus more if needed

FOR THE GRAVY:

1 cup (8 fl oz/250 ml)
chicken stock or beef
stock (page 110), or
prepared broth

1 tablespoon cornstarch
(cornflour)

¼ cup (2 fl oz/60 ml)
sherry

Salt and freshly ground
pepper

Using a sharp knife, cut a large pocket horizontally into each chop, slicing deep enough to touch the bone. Sprinkle the chops generously with salt and pepper, including inside the pocket.

Preheat the oven to 350°F (180°C).

In a large frying pan over medium heat, heat 2 tablespoons of the olive oil. Add the onion, garlic, celery, and sage and sauté until the onion is softened, 3–5 minutes. Stir in the bread crumbs and parsley and season to taste with salt and pepper. Sprinkle the bread-crumb mixture with the 1 tablespoon sherry and stir to combine. Add more sherry if needed so that all of the ingredients are moistened. Fill the pocket of each chop with one-fourth of the stuffing. Secure the pockets with wooden toothpicks or skewers.

In a large ovenproof frying pan or heavy casserole with a lid over medium-high heat, heat the remaining 2 tablespoons olive oil. When the oil is hot, add the chops and brown for 3–4 minutes on each side, turning carefully. Cover, transfer to the oven, and cook until the meat is light pink close to the bone and an instant-read thermometer inserted away from the bone registers 145°F (63°C), 12–15 minutes or longer. Transfer the chops to a platter and let them rest, tented loosely with aluminum foil.

To make the gravy, return the pan to medium-high heat. Add the chicken stock and deglaze the pan, scraping up any browned bits with a wooden spoon. Bring to a boil and cook until reduced by half. Mix the cornstarch with the sherry and add to the pan, season with salt and pepper, and cook, stirring, until thickened, 2–3 minutes more.

Transfer the chops to individual plates and serve with the hot sherry gravy.

MAKES 4 SERVINGS

SHERRY

A specialty of southwestern Spain, sherry is a fortified wine made from the Palomino grape. Sherry comes in eight different types, distinguished by color, flavor, sweetness, and alcohol content. The best known of these are pale gold, dry *fino*; very pale, very dry *manzanilla*; darker, slightly nutty, and dry to medium-dry *amontillado*; and mahogany brown sweet cream sherry. For this recipe, use an inexpensive semidry *amontillado* or dry *fino* sherry. (Do not use anything labeled "cooking sherry"; these are usually low-quality wines seasoned with salt and preservatives.)

17

GRILLED LAMB CHOPS WITH MINT-MASCARPONE PESTO

Slash the edges of the chops in 2 or 3 places to prevent curling. Season generously with salt and pepper and let stand at room temperature while you make the pesto.

To make the pesto, in a blender or food processor, combine the mint, mascarpone, pine nuts, and lemon juice and process until the mint is coarsely chopped. With the motor running, drizzle in the ¼ cup (2 fl oz/60 ml) olive oil and process until a loose paste is formed. Add a little more oil if necessary for the desired consistency. Season to taste with salt and pepper. Refrigerate while you grill the chops.

Prepare a charcoal or gas grill for direct grilling over medium-high heat (page 106). Grill the chops to the desired doneness, 3–5 minutes on each side. (Move to a cooler area of the grill if flare-ups occur.) Test for doneness by inserting an instant-read thermometer away from the bone or by cutting into the meat near the bone. Remove the chops from the grill when they are still quite pink near the bone for medium-rare (130°F/54°C). Transfer the chops to a platter and tent loosely with aluminum foil until ready to serve.

Spoon a liberal amount of the pesto onto individual plates and stack 2 chops, one on top of the other, on the pesto. Garnish with the mint sprigs and serve.

MAKES 4 SERVINGS

FRESH MINT
The mint family includes hundreds of species, but the variety most commonly used in the kitchen is spearmint, which has become a favorite herb of American cooks in recent years. Mint's lively aroma adds complexity to salsas and sauces and can be combined with oregano, thyme, rosemary, and other herbs in rubs and marinades. Fresh mint is both easily grown and widely available in the produce section of most markets.

8 lamb loin or rib chops, at least 1 inch (2.5 cm) thick, trimmed of excess fat

Salt and freshly ground pepper

FOR THE PESTO:

3 cups (3 oz/90 g) firmly packed fresh mint leaves

3 tablespoons mascarpone cheese

1 tablespoon pine nuts, toasted (page 114)

Juice of 1 lemon

¼ cup (2 fl oz/60 ml) olive oil, or more if needed

Fresh mint sprigs for garnish

GRILLED VEAL CHOPS WITH TARRAGON

FOR THE HERB PASTE:

**2 tablespoons chopped
fresh tarragon or
1 tablespoon dried**

2 or 3 cloves garlic, minced

1½ teaspoons salt

**1 teaspoon freshly ground
pepper**

**1 tablespoon olive oil,
plus more if needed**

**4 large veal loin chops, at
least 1 inch (2.5 cm) thick,
trimmed of excess fat**

Lemon wedges for garnish

**Fresh tarragon sprigs for
garnish**

To make the herb paste, in a small bowl, mix together the chopped tarragon, garlic to taste, salt, pepper, and the 1 tablespoon olive oil. Stir to make a coarse paste. Add a little more olive oil if needed.

Slash the edges of the chops in 1 or 2 places to prevent curling. Rub both sides of the chops generously with the herb paste and let stand at room temperature for at least 15 minutes or up to 1 hour, or cover and refrigerate overnight. Bring to room temperature, if necessary, before grilling.

Prepare a charcoal or gas grill for direct grilling over medium-high heat (page 106). Grill the chops until browned and grill-marked, 3–5 minutes on each side. Test for doneness by inserting an instant-read thermometer away from the bone or by cutting into the meat near the bone. Remove the chops from the grill just before the meat is done, when the center is pinkish and the temperature is 145°F (63°C). Transfer the chops to a platter and let rest, tented with aluminum foil, for 5 or 6 minutes before serving (the veal will continue to cook while resting).

Garnish the chops with lemon wedges and tarragon sprigs and serve 1 chop to each diner.

MAKES 4 SERVINGS

MAKING GRILL MARKS

Creating crosshatch grill marks is easy to do at home. Clean and oil the grill and prepare it for direct grilling over medium-high heat. Place the meat on the grill and sear for 2–3 minutes. Do not move the meat unless flare-ups occur. Turn the meat over and grill for another 2–3 minutes. Turn the meat over again, rotating it 90 degrees to make the crosshatch marks, and grill for another 2–3 minutes. Turn over and grill in the same position for another 2–3 minutes. If the meat needs to cook longer, move to a cooler part of the grill and cook, covered, to the desired doneness.

CHATEAUBRIAND WITH BÉARNAISE SAUCE

COOKING THICK STEAKS

Steaks thicker than 2 inches (5 cm) such as chateaubriand need special attention. With these thick cuts of tender meat, the aim is to cook the inside without charring the outside. First, sear the steak on both sides in a heavy frying pan to create an appetizing browned surface, and then finish by roasting it in an oven heated to 400° or 450°F (200° or 230°C). Or, if using a grill, stack the coals on one side to build a fire that is quite hot in one area and cooler in another. Sear the steak on both sides over the hottest area, then move it to a cooler area and cook, covered, until done.

To make the herb rub, in a small bowl, mix together the thyme, paprika, garlic powder, lemon pepper, and salt. Rub the beef with 1 tablespoon of the olive oil. Sprinkle the herb rub all over the beef. Let stand at room temperature for at least 15 minutes or up to 1 hour before cooking.

Preheat the oven to 400°F (200°C).

Coat the bottom of a large, heavy, ovenproof frying pan with the remaining 1 tablespoon oil and heat over high heat. Add the steak and sear on both sides until nicely browned, 3–5 minutes total. Transfer the pan to the oven and roast to the desired doneness, 10–20 minutes longer. Test for doneness using an instant-read thermometer or by cutting into the meat. Remove the steak from the oven when it is red at the center for rare (120°F/49°C) or deep pink at the center for medium-rare (130°F/54°C). Transfer to a carving board and let rest, tented loosely with aluminum foil, while you make the sauce.

To make the sauce, combine the wine, vinegar, shallot, tarragon, and ½ teaspoon pepper in a small saucepan and bring to a boil. Cook until reduced by two-thirds, 3–5 minutes. Transfer to a heat-proof bowl, stir in the lemon juice, and let cool. Place the bowl with the reduced wine mixture over a saucepan of simmering water (but not touching the water). Whisk the egg yolks into the wine mixture. Heat gently over the hot water, whisking constantly, until the mixture begins to thicken, 2–3 minutes. Remove from the heat and whisk in the butter to form a thick sauce. If it seems too thin, replace the bowl over the hot water and heat briefly, whisking constantly, until thickened. Season to taste with salt and pepper.

Slice the steak thickly on the diagonal across the grain and pass the sauce in a gravy boat. Serve with a helping of roasted potatoes.

MAKES 4 SERVINGS

FOR THE HERB RUB:

1½ teaspoons *each* dried thyme, paprika, and garlic powder

½ teaspoon lemon pepper (page 98)

¾ teaspoon salt

1 boneless top sirloin or beef fillet steak, about 2 lb (1 kg) and at least 2 inches (5 cm) thick, trimmed of excess fat

2 tablespoons olive oil

FOR THE BÉARNAISE SAUCE:

½ cup (4 oz/125 ml) dry white wine

1 tablespoon white wine vinegar

1 tablespoon finely chopped shallot

2 tablespoons chopped fresh tarragon or 1 tablespoon dried

Salt and ground pepper

Juice of ½ lemon

3 egg yolks, lightly beaten

½ cup (4 oz/125 g) unsalted butter, melted

Roasted potatoes for serving (page 111)

T-BONE STEAKS WITH
ROQUEFORT ROASTED TOMATOES

To prepare the steaks, trim any excess fat and slash the edges in 2 or 3 places to prevent curling. Brush the meat with the olive oil and rub all over with the crushed garlic. Sprinkle the steaks generously with salt and pepper. Let them stand at room temperature for at least 15 minutes or up to 1 hour, or cover and refrigerate overnight. Bring to room temperature for at least 45 minutes before grilling.

Preheat the oven to 400°F (200°C) and, if desired, prepare a grill for direct grilling over medium-high heat (page 106). (The broiler may be used in place of the grill.)

To make the roasted tomatoes, core the tomatoes with a small, sharp knife. With a large spoon, scoop out about 1 tablespoon of pulp from each tomato and discard. In a bowl, stir together the roquefort cheese and panko. Put 1 or 2 slices of garlic in each tomato cavity and spoon in the cheese mixture. Drizzle the olive oil on top. Place the tomatoes in a roasting pan and roast in the oven until the cheese is melted and the bread crumbs begin to brown, 5–7 minutes.

To make the creamed spinach, wash the spinach leaves well by immersing them in several changes of cold water. Put the spinach in a saucepan over medium-high heat with just the water clinging to the leaves. Cook, covered, until the spinach has wilted, about 5 minutes. Drain well in a colander, pressing on the spinach with the back of a spoon to remove excess moisture. Transfer the spinach to a cutting board, chop finely, and set aside.

In a large saucepan over medium heat, melt the butter. Add the chopped onion and sauté until translucent, 3–4 minutes. Slowly stir in the flour with a wooden spoon to make a roux. Cook, stirring, for about 1 minute. Whisk in the cream and continue

TENDER STEAKS
The most tender and flavorful steaks come from the short loin along the back of the steer. These include the tenderloin or beef fillet, a long, tender muscle that runs along the backbone; the New York steak, which is cut from the larger loin muscle; the porterhouse, which includes the loin and a large piece of fillet; and the T-bone, which is much like the porterhouse, but with a smaller fillet. Fillet steaks such as filet mignon and chateaubriand are boneless pieces cut from the tenderloin.

4 T-bone steaks, at least 1½ inches (4 cm) thick

1 tablespoon olive oil

4 cloves garlic, crushed

Salt and ground pepper

FOR THE TOMATOES:

4 large tomatoes

½ cup (2 oz/60 g) crumbled Roquefort or other blue cheese

½ cup (2 oz/60 g) panko or other dried bread crumbs (page 34)

1 clove garlic, sliced

1 tablespoon olive oil

FOR THE CREAMED SPINACH:

1 lb (500 g) fresh spinach, tough stems removed

2 tablespoons butter

2 tablespoons finely chopped onion or shallot

2 tablespoons all-purpose (plain) flour

1 cup (8 fl oz/250 ml) heavy (double) cream

¼ teaspoon freshly ground nutmeg

cooking until the mixture has thickened, 3–4 minutes. Add the nutmeg and stir. Add the chopped spinach and cook, stirring, until the sauce and spinach are combined and heated through, 3–4 minutes longer. Season to taste with salt and pepper.

Place the seasoned steaks on the prepared grill or in a broiler (grill), and cook to the desired doneness, about 3–5 minutes on each side. (Move to a cooler area of the grill, or farther from the heat in the broiler, if flare-ups occur.) Test for doneness using an instant-read thermometer or by cutting into the meat. Remove the steaks from the heat when they are red at the center for rare (120°F/49°C) or deep pink at the center for medium-rare (130°F/54°C). Transfer the steaks to a platter and let the meat rest for 5 minutes, tented loosely with aluminum foil, before serving.

Arrange each steak on an individual plate with a roasted tomato and a scoop of creamed spinach and serve.

MAKES 4 SERVINGS

(Photograph appears on following page.)

ROQUEFORT AND
OTHER BLUE CHEESES
Near the village of Roquefort in southern France are ancient caves where the world-famous Roquefort cheese is aged. A blue mold, *Penicillium roqueforti*, thrives there in the cool, damp atmosphere. The same species of mold is now used all over the world to create blue cheeses such as Stilton in England; Gorgonzola in Italy; and Wisconsin blue, Maytag blue, and others in the United States.

WEEKNIGHT MEALS

One great advantage of steaks and chops is that they are often fast and easy to prepare, just right for a weeknight dinner. But quick doesn't have to mean bland or boring. Try topping New York strip steak with blue cheese butter or lamb chops with tapenade—flavorful accompaniments that can be made ahead.

NEW YORK STRIP STEAK WITH
BLUE CHEESE BUTTER

COMPOUND BUTTERS

Compound, or flavored, butters are an easy way to add depth and sophistication to roasted or grilled meats. For garlic-herb butter, combine ½ cup (4 oz/125 g) softened butter, 1 teaspoon minced fresh thyme, ½ teaspoon minced fresh rosemary, and 1 head roasted garlic (page 111). For bourbon-mustard butter, combine ½ cup softened butter, 2 tablespoons Dijon mustard, and 1 tablespoon bourbon. Form the butters into logs, roll them up in parchment (baking) or waxed paper, twist the ends, and chill before slicing.

Slash the edges of the steaks in 2 or 3 places to prevent curling. In a small bowl, mix together the garlic powder and thyme and sprinkle all over the steaks. Sprinkle generously with salt and pepper. Let the steaks stand at room temperature for at least 15 minutes or up to 1 hour before cooking.

Preheat the broiler (grill) or prepare a gas or charcoal grill for direct grilling over medium-high heat (page 106).

In a bowl, mix together the butter and cheese. Transfer the mixture to a sheet of parchment (baking) or waxed paper and roll into a log. Twist the ends of the paper closed tightly and refrigerate the compound butter while you cook the steaks.

Broil or grill the steaks to the desired doneness, 3–5 minutes on each side. (Move the steaks away from the broiler flame or to a cooler area of the grill if flare-ups occur.) Test for doneness using an instant-read thermometer or by cutting into the meat. Remove the steaks from the heat when they are deep red at the center for rare (120°F/49°C) or deep pink at the center for medium-rare (130°F/54°C). Transfer the meat to a platter, tent loosely with aluminum foil, and let rest for 5 minutes before serving.

Serve with 1 or 2 pats of the blue cheese butter on each steak.

MAKES 4 SERVINGS

4 New York strip steaks, at least 1½ inches (4 cm) thick, trimmed of excess fat

1 tablespoon garlic powder

2 teaspoons dried thyme

Salt and freshly ground pepper

½ cup (4 oz/125 g) unsalted butter, at room temperature

¼ cup (1 oz/30 g) crumbled blue cheese

LONDON BROIL WITH RED WINE MARINADE

1 flank steak, about 2 lb (1 kg), trimmed of excess fat and silver skin

FOR THE MARINADE:

1 cup (8 fl oz/250 ml) dry red wine

2 tablespoons balsamic vinegar

¼ cup (1 oz/30 g) chopped yellow onion

2 tablespoons olive oil

1 tablespoon Worcestershire sauce

2 cloves garlic, minced

2 teaspoons minced fresh thyme or 1 teaspoon dried

2 bay leaves

2 teaspoons salt

1 teaspoon freshly ground pepper

Slash the steak across the grain in 2 or 3 places on both sides to prevent curling and place it in a shallow, nonreactive dish or large lock-top plastic bag.

To make the marinade, in a bowl, stir together the wine, vinegar, onion, olive oil, Worcestershire sauce, garlic, thyme, bay leaves, salt, and pepper. Pour the marinade over the steak. Cover the bowl or seal the bag and let it marinate at room temperature, turning the meat occasionally, for at least 15 minutes or up to 1 hour, or refrigerate overnight. Remove the steak from the marinade, pat dry, and let return to room temperature, if necessary, before cooking.

Preheat the broiler (grill) or prepare a gas or charcoal grill for direct grilling over medium-high heat (page 106).

Broil or grill the steak to the desired doneness, 3–5 minutes on each side. (Move the steak away from the broiler flame or to a cooler area of the grill if flare-ups occur.) Test for doneness using an instant-read thermometer or by cutting into the meat. Remove the steak from the heat when it is red at the center for rare (120°F/49°C) or deep pink at the center for medium-rare (130°F/54°C). Transfer the meat to a carving board and let rest for 5 minutes, tented loosely with aluminum foil, before serving.

Slice the steak thinly on the diagonal across the grain and serve.

MAKES 4 SERVINGS

MARINADES

Although marinades can help keep meats juicy and tender while cooking, their most important function is to add flavor. The longer you leave food in a marinade, the more the flavors penetrate. Cover steaks or chops with the marinade, turning them once or twice, and let sit for up to 1 hour at room temperature or overnight in the refrigerator. If you are using an acidic marinade such as the one for this recipe, be careful not to marinate tender meats such as pork tenderloins or fillet steaks for longer than 2 hours, or the meat can become mushy.

VEAL PICCATA

Preheat the oven to 150°F (65°C) and put a large baking dish in it.

Place the veal between 2 pieces of parchment (baking) paper or plastic wrap. Using a meat mallet or rolling pin, flatten the veal to an even thickness of about ¼ inch (6 mm). In a shallow bowl or deep plate, mix together the flour, 1 teaspoon salt, and 1 teaspoon pepper. In another bowl or plate, lightly beat the eggs with a few drops of water. Put the bread crumbs in a third bowl or plate. Dredge both sides of the veal pieces in the seasoned flour, then dip each piece in the beaten eggs and coat both sides thoroughly with the bread crumbs. Place the breaded veal on racks or plates.

In a large, heavy frying pan over medium-high heat, heat the olive oil. Add the veal pieces, in batches if necessary to avoid crowding, and fry until golden brown, about 1 minute on each side. Remove each piece from the pan as it is done and transfer to the baking dish in the oven to keep warm.

When all the veal is cooked, pour off all but 1 tablespoon of the oil from the pan. Add the wine and deglaze the pan, scraping up any browned bits from the bottom of the pan. Add the stock, lemon juice, and capers. Bring to a boil and cook, stirring often, until the sauce is reduced by half, about 5 minutes.

Transfer the veal cutlets to individual plates and serve with the pan sauce.

MAKES 4 SERVINGS

BREAD CRUMBS

When breading foods to create a crisp crust, dried bread crumbs work best. To make them at home, put stale bread slices in a low (200°F/95°C) oven until they become dry but not browned, 1 hour or longer. Let cool, then grate them using a box grater or process in a food processor to the desired consistency. Many chefs prefer to use the Japanese dried bread crumbs called panko, which make a uniform crunchy crust.

8–10 veal cutlets, about 1½ lb (750 g) total weight

1 cup (5 oz/155 g) all-purpose (plain) flour

Salt and freshly ground pepper

2 eggs

1 cup (4 oz/125 g) dried bread crumbs

3 tablespoons olive oil

½ cup (4 fl oz/125 ml) dry white wine

½ cup (4 fl oz/125 ml) chicken stock (page 110) or prepared broth

Juice of 1 lemon

1 tablespoon capers, rinsed and drained

LAMB CHOPS WITH TAPENADE

8 double-cut lamb loin
or rib chops, trimmed
of excess fat

Salt and freshly ground
pepper

FOR THE TAPENADE:

2 cups (10 oz/315 g) pitted
kalamata olives

1 cup (5 oz/155 g) pitted
green olives

4 cloves garlic, crushed

Zest and juice of 2 lemons

2 tablespoons coarsely
chopped fresh flat-leaf
(Italian) parsley

2 tablespoons olive oil

¼ cup (1 oz/30 g) dried
bread crumbs

2 tablespoons olive oil

Preheat the oven to 400°F (200°C).

Slash the fat ends of the chops in 1 or 2 places to prevent curling. Sprinkle generously with salt and pepper and set aside at room temperature for up to 1 hour.

To make the tapenade, in a food processor, combine the olives, garlic, lemon zest and juice, parsley, and 2 tablespoons olive oil. Pulse until the ingredients are incorporated but the mixture is still a bit chunky. Add the bread crumbs and pulse a few more times.

In a large ovenproof frying pan over medium-high heat, heat 2 tablespoons olive oil. When the oil just starts to smoke, add the lamb chops, in batches to avoid crowding, and sear them to a golden brown on all sides, about 4 minutes total. Pack a generous amount of the tapenade on the fat side of each chop and transfer the pan to the oven. Roast, tapenade side up, until an instant-read thermometer inserted away from the bone registers 130°–135°F (54–57°C) or the chops are pink when cut into near the bone for medium-rare, 6–8 minutes. Transfer the chops to a platter and let rest, tented loosely with foil, for 5 minutes.

Serve 2 chops per diner, topped with any extra tapenade.

MAKES 4 SERVINGS

OLIVES

Olives and their oil have been a part of Mediterranean cooking for thousands of years. Olives are grown in every Mediterranean country from Spain to the Levant and are used in cooking in myriad ways. They range in color from green to purple-black and are prepared by brining or curing in salt, herbs, and spices. Olives should be pitted (by hand or with a special olive pitter) before using in recipes. Many California and some imported olives, particularly the Greek kalamata, can be bought with the pits removed.

PORK CUTLETS WITH MARSALA-APRICOT SAUCE

GRINDING SPICES

Many home cooks are following the lead of professional chefs and grinding their own spices. Use a mortar and pestle to grind them by hand, or a small electric coffee grinder (keep it separate from the grinder you use for coffee). Place individual spices like peppercorns, star anise, cardamom seeds, cumin seeds, and fennel seeds or herbs such as bay leaves and rosemary in the grinder and process to the desired consistency. For a deeper flavor, toast the spices briefly in a hot pan, then let cool before grinding.

To make the rub, in a small bowl, mix together the paprika, onion powder, salt, five-spice powder, star anise, bay leaves, and cayenne. Slash the edges of the cutlets in 2 or 3 places to prevent curling. Sprinkle the spice rub all over the meat and let stand at room temperature for at least 15 minutes or up to 1 hour.

Coat the bottom of a large, heavy frying pan with the oil and heat over medium-high heat. Add the cutlets and cook until lightly browned, 2–3 minutes on each side. Reduce the heat to medium and cook for 5–7 minutes longer, turning once or twice. Test the meat for doneness using an instant-read thermometer or by cutting into the center of the meat. Pork loin is done when the internal temperature reaches 150°F (65°C); it should be slightly pink at the center. Remove from the heat just before the meat is done (145°F/63°C). Transfer to a platter and let rest, tented loosely with aluminum foil, while you make the sauce. (The pork will continue to cook while resting.)

To make the sauce, add ½ cup (4 fl oz/120 ml) of the Marsala to the pan and deglaze by scraping up any browned bits from the bottom. Stir in the chicken stock and apricots. Bring to a boil over high heat and cook, stirring often, until reduced by half, about 5 minutes. Stir in the apricot jam and lemon juice, reduce the heat to medium, and cook for 2–3 minutes longer, stirring often. Combine the cornstarch with the remaining ¼ cup (2 fl oz/60 ml) Marsala and stir into the sauce. Cook, stirring, until the sauce thickens slightly, about 3 minutes longer.

Transfer the cutlets to individual plates. Spoon some of the sauce over and serve. Pass additional sauce at the table.

MAKES 4 SERVINGS

FOR THE SPICE RUB:

1 tablespoon paprika

1 tablespoon onion powder

½ teaspoon salt

1 teaspoon Chinese five-spice powder (page 61)

1 teaspoon ground star anise or fennel seeds

½ teaspoon ground bay leaves

¼ teaspoon cayenne pepper

8 boneless pork loin cutlets, about 1 inch (2.5 cm) thick

1 tablespoon corn oil

FOR THE SAUCE:

¾ cup (6 fl oz/180 ml) dry Marsala or sherry

1 cup (8 fl oz/250 ml) chicken stock (page 110) or prepared broth

1 cup (6 oz/185 g) dried apricots, chopped

1 tablespoon apricot jam

Juice of ½ lemon

1 tablespoon cornstarch (cornflour)

PORK CHOPS WITH HARD CIDER PAN SAUCE

FOR THE SPICE RUB:

1 tablespoon paprika

1 tablespoon garlic powder

1 tablespoon onion powder

1 tablespoon dry mustard

1½ teaspoons salt

1 teaspoon freshly ground black pepper

¼ teaspoon cayenne pepper

8 bone-in pork loin or rib chops, about 1 inch (2.5 cm) thick, trimmed of excess fat

1 tablespoon olive oil

FOR THE PAN SAUCE:

1 cup (8 fl oz/250 ml) hard cider or apple juice

¼ cup (2 oz/60 g) Dijon or Creole mustard

1 tablespoon Worcestershire sauce

1 tablespoon tomato paste

1 or 2 dashes of Tabasco or other hot-pepper sauce

¼ cup (2 fl oz/60 ml) heavy (double) cream

To make the spice rub, in a small bowl, mix together the paprika, garlic powder, onion powder, dry mustard, salt, black pepper, and cayenne. Slash the edges of the chops in 2 or 3 places to prevent curling. Sprinkle the rub all over the chops and let stand at room temperature for at least 15 minutes or up to 1 hour.

Coat the bottom of a large, heavy frying pan with the olive oil and heat over medium-high heat. Add the chops, in batches if necessary to avoid crowding, and cook until lightly browned, about 3 minutes on each side. Reduce the heat to medium and cook for 5–7 minutes longer, turning once or twice. Test the meat for doneness by inserting an instant-read thermometer away from the bone or by cutting into the meat close to the bone. Remove from the heat just before the meat is done, when the internal temperature is 145°F (63°C). (Pork loin is done when it reaches 150°F/65°C, but it will continue to cook while resting.) Transfer to a platter and let rest, tented loosely with aluminum foil, while you prepare the pan sauce.

To make the pan sauce, add the cider to the same pan and deglaze by scraping up any browned bits from the bottom. Bring to a boil and cook, stirring often, until reduced by half, about 5 minutes. Reduce the heat to medium and whisk in the Dijon mustard, Worcestershire sauce, tomato paste, and Tabasco. Cook for 2–3 minutes longer, whisking often. Remove from the heat and whisk in the cream. Taste and adjust the seasoning.

Transfer the chops to individual plates. Spoon some of the sauce over the chops and serve. Pass additional sauce at the table.

MAKES 4 SERVINGS

HARD CIDER

Johnny Appleseed wasn't spreading apples through the Midwest just so settlers could make apple pie. Hard cider was the beverage of choice for many early Americans. Apple juice with a kick and a bit of fizz left from fermentation is an ancient tradition. Delicious hard cider called *scrumpy* is made in southern England; French *cidre* accompanies the local cuisine in Normandy; and fine hard ciders are also produced by American and Canadian apple growers, many of whom use heirloom cider apples. Choose any of these types of cider for this recipe.

ELEGANT OCCASIONS

Steaks and chops paired with a rich sauce, a lustrous glaze, or an aromatic oil make a dramatic cornerstone for an elegant dinner party. Tender beef fillet flavored with truffle oil, lamb and veal chops with rich sauces based on port or wild mushrooms, or pork tenderloin with an orange-scented glaze will set the stage for a memorable evening.

FILETS MIGNONS WITH
BALSAMIC PAN SAUCE AND TRUFFLE OIL
44

FILLET TIPS ON ROSEMARY SKEWERS
47

LAMB CHOPS WITH PORT SAUCE
48

PAN-ROASTED PORK TENDERLOIN
WITH GRAND MARNIER GLAZE
51

VEAL CUTLETS WITH WILD MUSHROOMS
52

VEAL CHOPS MILANESE WITH SAFFRON RISOTTO
55

FILETS MIGNONS WITH
BALSAMIC PAN SAUCE AND TRUFFLE OIL

Sprinkle the steaks generously with salt and pepper.

Coat the bottom of a large, heavy frying pan with the olive oil and heat over medium-high heat. Add the steaks and cook to the desired doneness, 3–5 minutes on each side. Test for doneness using an instant-read thermometer or by cutting into the meat. Remove the steaks from the heat when they are red at the center for rare (120°F/52°C) or deep pink at the center for medium-rare (130°F/54°C). Transfer to a platter and let rest, tented loosely with aluminum foil, while you make the sauce.

In the same pan over medium-high heat, add the vinegar and deglaze by scraping up any browned bits from the bottom. Cook until slightly reduced and thickened, about 3 minutes. Remove from the heat. Whisk in the butter to form a smooth sauce.

To serve, transfer the steaks to individual plates, top with the sauce, and drizzle with a small amount of the truffle oil.

MAKES 4 SERVINGS

4 filet mignon steaks, at least 1½ inches (4 cm) thick

Salt and freshly ground pepper

1 tablespoon olive oil

¼ cup (2 fl oz/60 ml) balsamic vinegar

2 tablespoons unsalted butter

Truffle oil for drizzling

TRUFFLE OIL

You can find many flavored oils on the market, from lemon- and orange-infused oil to Asian hot chile oil. But the most elegant and prized among them is truffle oil. Flavored with the essence of aromatic wild fungi found in Italy and southern France, this oil contributes an almost indescribable earthiness and complexity to meat dishes. Truffle oil should be used sparingly, lest its strong flavor overwhelm everything else on the plate.

FILLET TIPS ON ROSEMARY SKEWERS

2 fillet tips or other pieces of beef fillet, about 2 lb (1 kg) total weight, cut into ¾-inch (2-cm) chunks

8 large rosemary stems, stripped and trimmed to a point, or wooden skewers, soaked in water for at least 30 minutes

FOR THE ROSEMARY RUB:

1 tablespoon garlic powder

2 teaspoons onion powder

1 tablespoon chopped fresh rosemary or 1½ teaspoons dried

2 teaspoons salt

1 teaspoon freshly ground pepper

Preheat the broiler (grill) or prepare a charcoal or gas grill for direct grilling over medium-high heat (page 106).

Thread the chunks of fillet onto the rosemary skewers, leaving a little space between the chunks.

To make the rub, in a small bowl, mix together the garlic powder, onion powder, rosemary, salt, and pepper. Sprinkle the rub all over the meat. Let the skewers stand at room temperature for at least 15 minutes or up to 1 hour.

Grill the skewers to the desired doneness, 4–7 minutes on each side. Test for doneness by using an instant-read thermometer or by cutting into the meat. Remove from the heat when it is red at the center for rare (120°F/49°C) or deep pink at the center for medium-rare (130°F/54°C). Let the skewers rest for 5 minutes. Serve each diner 2 skewers on warmed individual plates.

MAKES 4 SERVINGS

USING SKEWERS

Cooking food on skewers or sticks over a fire is an ancient technique. Virtually every cuisine features some kind of skewered meat, from the county fair's corn dog to Japanese *yaki-tori* (marinated and grilled chicken). If you use wooden skewers, soak them for 30 minutes or longer before using so they won't burn. Using the stripped stems of rosemary, as in this recipe, adds extra flavor to the skewered foods.

LAMB CHOPS WITH PORT SAUCE

Preheat the oven to 400°F (200°C).

Slash the edges of the chops in 2 or 3 places to prevent curling. Sprinkle generously with salt and pepper.

Coat the bottom of a large, ovenproof frying pan with the olive oil and heat over medium-high heat. When the oil starts to smoke, add the lamb chops and sear them to a golden brown on both sides, about 2 minutes on each side. (Do not crowd the pan; use 2 frying pans if necessary.) Transfer the pan(s) to the oven and roast until an instant-read thermometer inserted away from the bone registers 130°–135°F (54°–57°C) or the chops are deep pink when cut into near the bone for medium-rare, 6–8 minutes. Transfer to a platter and let rest, tented loosely with aluminum foil, while you make the sauce.

To make the sauce, drain off all but 1 tablespoon of drippings from the pan. Add the shallots and garlic and sauté, stirring often, until softened, 3–4 minutes. Add the Port and stock and bring to a boil over high heat. Cook until reduced by half, about 5 minutes. Reduce the heat to medium. Whisk in the mustard and then the butter pieces. When the butter has melted and combined and the sauce is smooth, season to taste with salt and pepper.

Transfer the chops to individual plates, spoon the sauce on top, and serve.

MAKES 4 SERVINGS

PORT STYLES

Sweet, fortified wines such as Port, which are made by adding brandy to fermenting grapes, give a touch of sweetness and complexity to sauces, balancing acidic components such as tomatoes or citrus. Port traditionally comes from the Douro region of Portugal, but similar wines are now produced in other regions such as California and Australia. Ruby Port is sweet and strong and usually has a fruity character. Aged tawny Port has a softer flavor and brownish tinge. Save the more expensive vintage Port for drinking, not cooking.

8 double-cut lamb loin or rib chops, trimmed of excess fat

Salt and freshly ground pepper

1 tablespoon olive oil

FOR THE PORT SAUCE:

2 shallots, minced

2 cloves garlic, minced

2 cups (16 fl oz/500 ml) ruby Port

1 cup (8 fl oz/250 ml) beef stock (page 110) or prepared broth

1 teaspoon Dijon mustard

1 tablespoon chilled unsalted butter, cut into pieces

Salt and freshly ground pepper

PAN-ROASTED PORK TENDERLOIN
WITH GRAND MARNIER GLAZE

2 pork tenderloins, about 1½ lb (750 g) each

1 cup (8 fl oz/250 ml) fresh orange juice

¼ cup (2 fl oz/60 ml) Grand Marnier

2 tablespoons dry mustard

2 cloves garlic, minced

1 tablespoon peeled and chopped fresh ginger

2 tablespoons *each* **soy sauce and rice vinegar**

1 teaspoon Asian hot-pepper sauce

½ teaspoon vanilla extract (essence)

FOR THE GLAZE:

¼ cup (2 fl oz/60 ml) Grand Marnier

3 tablespoons Dijon mustard

2 teaspoons grated orange zest

½ teaspoon lemon pepper (page 98)

1 tablespoon olive oil

Orange-mint relish for serving *(far right)*

Cut the tenderloins in half crosswise to form 4 small roasts and place them in a shallow, nonreactive dish. In a bowl, stir together the orange juice, ¼ cup Grand Marnier, dry mustard, garlic, ginger, soy sauce, vinegar, hot-pepper sauce, and vanilla. Pour the mixture over the pork. Cover and marinate at room temperature for at least 15 minutes or up to 1 hour. Remove the pork and pat dry. Strain the marinade through a fine-mesh sieve and reserve ½ cup (4 fl oz/125 ml).

Preheat the oven to 400°F (200°C).

To make the glaze, in a small saucepan, whisk together ¼ cup Grand Marnier, Dijon mustard, reserved strained marinade, orange zest, and lemon pepper. Bring to a boil over high heat and cook until reduced by half, about 5 minutes. Set aside and let cool.

Coat the bottom of a large, ovenproof frying pan with the olive oil and heat over medium-high heat. Add the pork and sear, turning often, until browned on all sides, about 5 minutes. (Do not crowd the pan.) Transfer the pan to the oven and roast the pork for about 10–12 minutes. Brush the pork often with the glaze for the last 5 minutes of cooking. Test for doneness by inserting an instant-read thermometer or by cutting into the meat. Pork tenderloin is done when the internal temperature reaches 150°F (65°C); it should be slightly pink in the center. Remove from the heat just before the meat is done (145°F/63°C). Brush the pork thoroughly once more with the glaze and let rest, loosely tented with aluminum foil, for 5–10 minutes. (The pork will continue to cook while resting.)

Arrange the pork tenderloins on individual plates and serve with the relish on the side.

MAKES 4 SERVINGS

ORANGE-MINT RELISH

In a bowl, mix together 2 seedless oranges, peeled, halved, and thinly sliced; 1 Walla Walla or other sweet onion, halved and thinly sliced; ½ cup (¾ oz/20 g) chopped fresh mint; and 2 tablespoons peeled and chopped fresh ginger. In a small bowl, whisk together 3 tablespoons vegetable oil with 1 tablespoon *each* rice vinegar and soy sauce. Pour the vinaigrette over the orange mixture and toss to combine.

VEAL CUTLETS WITH WILD MUSHROOMS

Place the veal cutlets between 2 pieces of parchment (baking) paper or plastic wrap. Using a meat mallet or rolling pin, flatten the cutlets to an even thickness of about ¼ inch (6 mm). In a shallow bowl or deep plate, mix together the flour, paprika, tarragon, 2 teaspoons salt, and 1 teaspoon pepper. Dredge the veal on both sides in the seasoned flour, shake off the excess, and set aside.

In a large frying pan, melt the 1 tablespoon butter with the olive oil over medium-high heat. When the butter is foaming, add the veal, in batches to avoid crowding, and sauté, turning once or twice, until lightly browned on both sides, 5–6 minutes. Transfer the cutlets to a platter and tent loosely with aluminum foil to keep them warm.

Add more butter if needed and add the mushrooms to the pan. Sauté, stirring often, until softened and lightly browned, 4–5 minutes. Stir in the sherry, stock, and tomato paste. Raise the heat to high and cook, stirring often, until the sauce thickens, 3–5 minutes. Remove from the heat and stir in the cream, if using.

Transfer the veal to individual plates and top with the mushroom sauce. Serve at once.

MAKES 4 SERVINGS

MUSHROOM VARIETIES

Cooks can now choose from a dazzling array of mushrooms. In addition to the common white variety, you'll find small brown cremini mushrooms and the large mature version of the same mushroom, portobellos. Many markets stock flavorful Asian shiitakes; tiny straw mushrooms, also called *enoki;* and delicate oyster mushrooms, as well as fresh wild mushrooms such as king boletes, also called porcini or ceps; yellow and black chanterelles; morels; wood ear fungi; and the fragrant *matsutake,* or pine mushroom.

8 veal cutlets, about 1½ lb (750 g) total weight

1 cup (5 oz/155 g) all-purpose (plain) flour

1 tablespoon paprika

1 tablespoon dried tarragon

Salt and freshly ground pepper

1 tablespoon unsalted butter, plus more if needed

1 tablespoon olive oil

1 lb (500 g) wild mushrooms such as chanterelles, porcini (ceps), morels, shiitakes, or a combination, brushed clean and chopped

¼ cup (2 fl oz/60 ml) sherry or Marsala

½ cup (4 oz/125 g) chicken stock or veal stock (page 110) or prepared broth

2 tablespoons tomato paste

2 tablespoons heavy (double) cream or sour cream (optional)

VEAL CHOPS MILANESE WITH SAFFRON RISOTTO

4 thin bone-in or boneless veal chops, about 1½ lb (750 g) total weight

Salt and freshly ground pepper

3 cups (24 fl oz/750 ml) chicken stock (page 110)

½ cup (4 fl oz/125 ml) dry white wine

½ teaspoon saffron threads *(far right),* crushed

2 tablespoons unsalted butter or olive oil

½ yellow onion, finely chopped

1 cup (7 oz/220 g) Arborio or Carnaroli rice

½ cup (2 oz/60 g) freshly grated Parmesan cheese

1 cup (5 oz/155 g) fresh or thawed frozen peas

Olive oil for frying

1 cup (5 oz/155 g) all-purpose (plain) flour

2 eggs

1 cup (4 oz/125 g) dried bread crumbs

2 teaspoons dried oregano

Lemon wedges for serving

Slash the edges of the chops in 2 or 3 places to prevent curling. Place the veal between 2 pieces of parchment (baking) paper or plastic wrap. Using a meat mallet, and avoiding the bone, if necessary, flatten the veal to an even thickness of about ¼ inch (6 mm). Sprinkle with salt and pepper and set aside.

In a saucepan over medium-high heat, combine the stock, wine, and saffron. Bring to a boil, stirring occasionally. Reduce the heat to medium-low and keep at a slow simmer.

In a large, heavy saucepan, melt the butter over medium heat. Add the onion and sauté until translucent, 5–7 minutes. Stir in the rice and cook, stirring often, until well coated, 2–3 minutes. Stir in ½ cup (4 fl oz/125 ml) of the stock mixture and cook, stirring often, until the liquid is absorbed. Keep adding the stock in ½-cup increments, stirring until the rice is al dente (tender but slightly chewy), about 20 minutes. Reduce the heat to low and stir in the cheese and peas; cook until the peas are tender, 2–3 minutes longer. Season to taste with salt and pepper.

When the risotto is almost done, pour olive oil to a depth of ½ inch (12 mm) in a large frying pan and heat over medium-high heat. Put the flour in a shallow bowl. In another bowl, lightly beat the eggs with a few drops of water. In a third bowl, stir together the bread crumbs and oregano. Dredge each veal chop first in the flour, then in the egg, and finally coating thoroughly with the bread crumbs. Add the chops to the pan, in batches if necessary to avoid crowding, and fry until both sides are golden brown and the meat is just cooked through, 2–3 minutes on each side. Transfer to a plate lined with paper towels to drain.

Transfer the chops to individual plates along with a scoop of the risotto, garnish with lemon wedges, and serve.

MAKES 4 SERVINGS

SAFFRON

The orange-red stamens of the *Crocus sativa* flower, saffron is among the most treasured spices in the world. More than 70 thousand flowers must be picked and their stamens removed by hand to produce 1 pound (500 g) of saffron. Yet the distinctive earthy flavor and rich gold color make it worth its high price. It is used in many recipes, including the bouillabaisse of southern France and in this classic Italian risotto. The threadlike stamens are sold in small quantities and should be soaked in hot liquid before use to bring out their flavor.

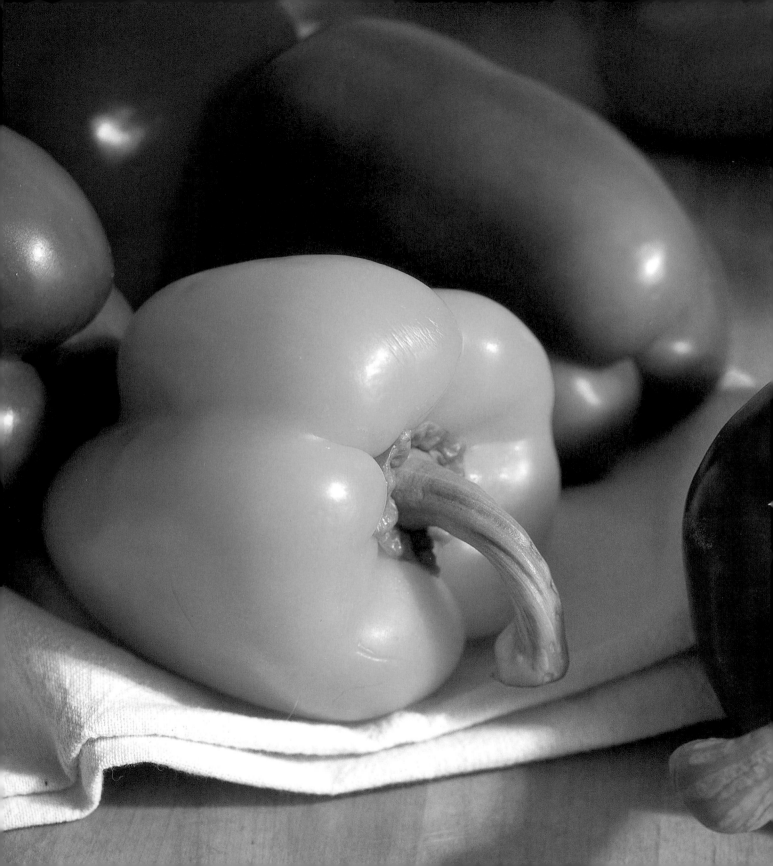

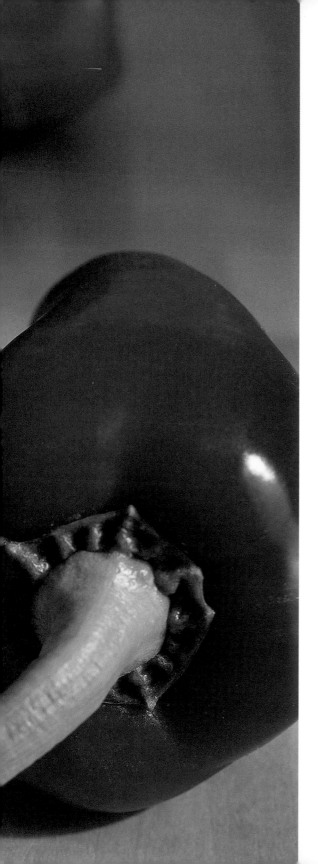

SUMMER GRILLING

When the sun comes out and it is time to fire up the grill, steaks and chops are the perfect choice. Don't limit yourself to just old favorites. Try new combinations such as beef tri-tip coated with Chinese spices and served with grilled-pineapple barbecue sauce, or a thick porterhouse steak grilled the Florentine way.

BISTECCA FIORENTINA WITH LEMON SPINACH
58

FIVE-SPICE GINGER TRI-TIP
WITH PINEAPPLE BARBECUE SAUCE
61

GRILLED SKIRT STEAK FAJITAS
WITH TEQUILA MARINADE
62

VEAL CHOPS WITH FIRE-ROASTED BELL PEPPERS
AND TOMATOES
65

PORK RIBS WITH PINEAPPLE-HOISIN GLAZE
66

BUTTERFLIED PORK TENDERLOIN
WITH CHIPOTLE-OREGANO CRUST
69

LAMB CHOPS GRILLED IN ROSEMARY SMOKE
70

BISTECCA FIORENTINA WITH LEMON SPINACH

GRILLING TIPS

For best results when grilling, first ignite the charcoal using a chimney starter or lighter fluid. Pile two-thirds of the hot coals in one part of the grill and the remaining one-third in another, leaving one area without any coals. For a gas grill, turn one burner to high, turn one to medium, and leave one turned off. When cooking thick steaks or chops, first sear both sides over medium-high heat, then transfer to the medium- or low-heat area to continue cooking, covered, until done. For more information on grilling, see page 106.

Slash the edges of the steaks in 1 or 2 places to prevent curling. Rub the steaks all over with olive oil and rub the garlic over both sides of each steak. Sprinkle generously with salt and pepper.

Prepare a charcoal or gas grill for grilling over medium-high heat *(left)*. Brush off any excess garlic from the steaks and sear over the hot area of the grill, 3–4 minutes on each side. Move the steaks to a cooler area of the grill, cover, and cook to the desired doneness, turning once, 5–7 minutes on each side. Test for doneness using an instant-read thermometer or by cutting into the meat. Remove the steaks from the heat when they are red at the center for rare (120°F/49°C) or deep pink at the center for medium-rare (130°F/54°C). Transfer to a carving board and let rest, loosely tented with aluminum foil, while you prepare the spinach.

To make the lemon spinach, wash the spinach in several changes of cold water. In a large frying pan over medium-high heat, heat the olive oil. Add the spinach with just the water clinging to the leaves. Sprinkle with the lemon juice, stir, and cover. Cook until wilted, 2–3 minutes. Remove from the heat and season to taste with salt and pepper.

Slice the steaks thickly on the diagonal across the grain. Arrange on individual plates with the sautéed spinach and garnish with the lemon slices.

*Note: In Tuscany, where this dish originates, it is always served very rare (*al sangue, *or "bloody," in Italian). Asking a Florentine chef to cook a bistecca medium is tantamount to asking a sushi chef to charbroil your sashimi.*

MAKES 4 SERVINGS

2 porterhouse steaks, at least 2 inches (5 cm) thick, trimmed of excess fat

1 tablespoon olive oil, or more as needed

4 cloves garlic, crushed

Salt and freshly ground pepper

FOR THE LEMON SPINACH:

1 lb (500 g) spinach, tough stems removed

2 tablespoons olive oil

Juice of ½ lemon

Salt and freshly ground pepper

Lemon slices for garnish

FIVE-SPICE GINGER TRI-TIP WITH PINEAPPLE BARBECUE SAUCE

FOR THE SPICE RUB:

1 tablespoon Chinese
five-spice powder

2 teaspoons garlic powder

2 teaspoons onion powder

2 teaspoons salt

1 teaspoon ground ginger

½ teaspoon cayenne
pepper

½ pineapple, peeled, cored
(page 115), and sliced into
½-inch (12-mm) rounds

1 tri-tip roast, 2–3 lb
(1–1.5 kg), trimmed of
excess fat

2 cups (16 oz/500 g)
ketchup

1 cup (8 oz/250 g)
Chinese-style hot mustard

1 bottle (12 fl oz/375 ml)
ale or medium-bodied beer

¼ cup (2 fl oz/60 ml)
Worcestershire sauce

2 tablespoons soy sauce

1 tablespoon garlic powder

1 tablespoon onion powder

2 teaspoons Asian
hot-pepper sauce

To make the spice rub, in a small bowl, mix together the five-spice powder, garlic powder, onion powder, salt, ginger, and cayenne. Rub the meat all over with the spice rub and let it sit at room temperature for at least 15 minutes or up to 1 hour before cooking.

Prepare a charcoal or gas grill for grilling over medium-high heat (page 106). Arrange the pineapple pieces over direct heat and grill until caramelized, 2–3 minutes per side. Transfer the pineapple to a platter and let cool. Slash the top of the roast in 2 or 3 places to prevent curling. Place over direct heat and sear on all sides, 3–5 minutes on each side. Move to a cooler area of the grill and cook, covered, 15 minutes longer.

While the roast is cooking, cut the cooled pineapple into ½-inch (12-mm) dice. In a large saucepan over high heat, combine the ketchup, mustard, ale, Worcestershire sauce, soy sauce, garlic powder, onion powder, and hot-pepper sauce and bring to a boil. Reduce the heat to medium-low and simmer the sauce until thickened to the consistency of ketchup, about 15 minutes. Add the diced pineapple and cook until heated through, 1–2 minutes longer. Transfer to a food processor and purée.

Check the roast for doneness with an instant-read thermometer. The temperature should be 120°–130°F (49°–54°C) for rare to medium-rare, and the meat should be red or dark pink near the center. Transfer to a platter and baste generously with the sauce. Let rest, tented loosely with aluminum foil, for 5–10 minutes.

Slice the meat thickly on the diagonal across the grain and serve, topping the slices with the sauce.

Note: You will have extra barbecue sauce left over for another use.

MAKES 4–6 SERVINGS

CHINESE FIVE-SPICE POWDER

The number five is lucky in Chinese culture and has always been considered a good number for a mixture of medicinal herbs. However, there are not always five spices in Chinese five-spice powder. The blend of this popular Asian flavoring usually includes fennel seed, star anise, Sichuan pepper, cloves, cinnamon, and dried ginger. Five-spice powder is sold at Asian groceries and well-stocked supermarkets.

GRILLED SKIRT STEAK FAJITAS WITH TEQUILA MARINADE

To make the marinade, in a bowl, stir together the lime juice, orange juice, beer, tequila (if using), cilantro, and jalapeño. Place the steak in a shallow, nonreactive dish or large lock-top plastic bag. Pour the marinade over the meat. Cover or seal and marinate at room temperature for at least 15 minutes or up to 1 hour, turning occasionally. Remove the steak from the marinade and pat dry.

Preheat the broiler (grill) or prepare a charcoal or gas grill for cooking over medium-high heat (page 106).

In a large frying pan over medium-high heat, heat the olive oil. Add the bell peppers, onion, and garlic and sauté until the onion is translucent and the peppers are softened, 5–7 minutes. Set aside.

Broil or grill the skirt steak to the desired doneness, 3–4 minutes on each side. Test for doneness by inserting an instant-read thermometer or by cutting into the meat. Remove the steak from the heat when it is red at the center for rare (120°F/49°C) or deep pink at the center for medium-rare (130°F/54°C). Let the steak rest for 5 minutes, tented loosely with aluminum foil.

Slice the steak thinly on the diagonal across the grain and serve on the tortillas with a liberal heap of the bell peppers and onion.

MAKES 4 SERVINGS

JULIENNING

Cutting vegetables into a matchstick shape called julienne produces a pleasing uniform look. First cut the vegetables into equal rectangular pieces about ¼ inch (6 mm) thick, 2 inches (5 cm) long, and 1 inch (2.5 cm) wide. Cut again along the 2-inch length to produce uniform ¼-inch pieces. Julienned vegetables add color and texture to soups and salads; in this recipe they are sautéed as an essential component of savory fajitas.

FOR THE MARINADE:

Juice of 3 limes

Juice of 2 oranges

1 bottle (12 fl oz/375 ml) Mexican beer

3 tablespoons tequila (optional)

1 tablespoon finely chopped fresh cilantro (fresh coriander)

1 jalapeño chile, seeded and coarsely chopped

1 skirt steak, about 1½ lb (750 g), trimmed of excess fat and cut into 4 pieces

2 tablespoons olive oil

1 *each* red, yellow, and green bell pepper (capsicum), cut into julienne *(far left)*

1 red onion, thinly sliced

2 cloves garlic, minced

Warmed corn or flour tortillas for serving

VEAL CHOPS WITH FIRE-ROASTED BELL PEPPERS AND TOMATOES

4 veal loin chops, at least 1 inch (2.5 cm) thick, trimmed of excess fat

1 tablespoon olive oil, plus extra for drizzling

FOR THE SAGE RUB:

2 tablespoons dried sage

2 tablespoons paprika

2 tablespoons garlic powder

1½ teaspoons salt

1½ teaspoons lemon pepper (page 98)

½ teaspoon cayenne pepper

4 large, ripe tomatoes

2 yellow bell peppers (capsicums), roasted *(far right),* and cut into thin strips

Slash the edges of the chops in 1 or 2 places to prevent curling. Rub them with the 1 tablespoon olive oil.

To make the rub, in a small bowl, mix together the sage, paprika, garlic powder, salt, lemon pepper, and cayenne. Rub the meat all over with the rub, reserving 1 tablespoon. Let the veal stand at room temperature for 15 minutes or up to 1 hour before cooking.

Prepare a charcoal or gas grill for cooking over medium-high heat (page 106). Grill the chops, turning once, until browned and grill-marked (page 21), 3–5 minutes on each side. Test for doneness using an instant read thermometer or by cutting into the meat near the bone; cook longer if needed. Veal is done when the internal temperature registers 150°F (65°C) and the meat is slightly pink and very juicy. Remove the chops from the grill when the thermometer reaches 145°F (63°C). Let them rest, tented with aluminum foil, for 5 minutes. (The chops will continue to cook while resting.)

While the chops are cooking, core the tomatoes and cut in half. Drizzle the cut sides with olive oil and sprinkle with the reserved 1 tablespoon herb rub. Arrange on the grill, cut sides down, over medium-high heat and sear until grill-marked, about 2 minutes. Do not overcook. Remove from the heat and set aside.

Place the roasted peppers on a platter, arrange the veal chops and grilled tomatoes on top, and serve at once.

MAKES 4 SERVINGS

FIRE-ROASTING PEPPERS

Bell peppers are delicious when roasted over an open flame. The trick is to blister and char them over high heat, whether a grill or the gas flame of a stove, using tongs to turn the them until blackened on all sides. Transfer to a paper bag and seal for a few minutes. Then remove the skin with your fingers—it should come off easily. Use a paring knife to remove stubborn bits. Then split open the peppers and remove the seeds and membranes.

PORK RIBS WITH PINEAPPLE-HOISIN GLAZE

COOKING PORK RIBS

Most markets offer three types of pork ribs for sale. Baby back ribs, which are featured in this recipe, are cut from the loin. These are the most tender, and they cook in about 2 hours. Country-style ribs are cut from the shoulder and can be cooked the same way, or they can be grilled by first searing over medium-high heat and then roasting indirectly over low to medium heat, at 325°F (165°C) for 2 hours or longer. Spareribs are cut from the belly and require long, slow cooking, 2–3 hours or more.

Preheat the oven to 250°F (120°C).

Season the ribs generously with the pepper and five-spice powder. (Hoisin sauce is salty, so the ribs will most likely not need additional salt.) Wrap each piece of meat in heavy-duty aluminum foil. Place the foil-wrapped ribs on a baking sheet or in a shallow roasting pan and roast for 1 hour.

Prepare a charcoal or gas grill for indirect cooking over medium-low heat (page 106).

To make the glaze, stir together the hoisin sauce, pineapple juice, vinegar, and sesame oil in a saucepan. Bring just to a simmer over medium heat; do not let boil. Simmer, stirring frequently, until reduced to the consistency of ketchup, about 15 minutes. Remove the mixture from the heat and add the brown sugar. Stir until the sugar dissolves.

Remove the ribs from the oven, unwrap, and place them on the cooler part of the grill. Grill, covered, turning every 10 minutes or so, until tender and browned, about 1 hour. During the last 20 minutes of grilling, leave the meaty side of the ribs up and baste every 5 minutes with the glaze. Remove the ribs from the heat, baste once more, and wrap in clean heavy-duty aluminum foil. Let rest for 10–12 minutes.

Slice the racks along the bones and divide among individual plates. Spoon any leftover glaze over the ribs, and serve at once.

MAKES 4 SERVINGS

2 racks baby back ribs, about 5 lb (2.5 kg) total weight, each rack trimmed of excess fat and cut into 2 pieces

1 tablespoon freshly ground pepper

3 tablespoons Chinese five-spice powder (page 61)

FOR THE GLAZE:

1½ cups (12 fl oz/375 ml) hoisin sauce

2 cups (16 fl oz/500 ml) pineapple juice

1 tablespoon rice wine vinegar

2 teaspoons sesame oil

1 teaspoon firmly packed brown sugar

BUTTERFLIED PORK TENDERLOIN WITH CHIPOTLE-OREGANO CRUST

FOR THE CHILE PASTE:

2 canned chipotle chiles in adobo sauce *(far right)*

2 cloves garlic

2 tablespoons tomato paste

2 tablespoons corn oil

1 teaspoon salt

2 pork tenderloins, each about 1½ lb (750 g)

2 tablespoons dried oregano

FOR THE CHIPOTLE GRAVY:

2 cups (16 fl oz/500 ml) chicken stock (page 110) or prepared broth

1 tablespoon Worcestershire sauce

1 teaspoon sugar

1 teaspoon red wine vinegar

1 tablespoon cornstarch (cornflour) mixed with ¼ cup (2 fl oz/60 ml) sweet vermouth

To make the chile paste, in a food processor, combine the chiles with their sauce, garlic, tomato paste, oil, and salt and purée.

Cut each tenderloin crosswise into 2 pieces. Butterfly each of the pieces by cutting lengthwise down the center, stopping about ½ inch (12 mm) from the other side. Place each piece between 2 pieces of parchment (baking) paper or plastic wrap and use a meat mallet or rolling pin to flatten to an even thickness of ¾ inch (2 cm). Rub the meat with the chile paste, reserving ¼ cup (2 oz/60 g). Sprinkle with the oregano. Let the pork stand at room temperature for at least 15 minutes or up to 1 hour before cooking.

Prepare a charcoal or gas grill for direct grilling over medium-high heat (page 106). Grill the tenderloins over direct heat, covered, turning once or twice, for about 10 minutes total. (Move to the cooler area of the grill if flare-ups occur.) Test for doneness using an instant-read thermometer or by cutting into the meat at the thickest part. Pork tenderloin is done when the internal temperature is 150°F (65°C); it should be slightly pink in the center. Remove the pork from the heat at 145°F (63°C) and let rest, tented with aluminum foil. (The pork will continue to cook while resting.)

To make the gravy, in a saucepan over high heat, whisk together the stock, reserved chile paste, Worcestershire sauce, sugar, and vinegar. Bring to a boil and cook until reduced by half, about 5 minutes. Reduce the heat to medium-low and whisk in the cornstarch mixture. Cook, stirring often, until slightly thickened, about 5 minutes. Remove from the heat and strain through a fine-mesh sieve.

Serve the tenderloins on individual plates, topped with the gravy.

MAKES 4 SERVINGS

CHIPOTLE CHILES

Chipotles are red jalapeño chiles that have been dried and smoked. They are often sold canned in adobo sauce, a spicy mixture of tomato and vinegar. Canned chipotles lend a piquancy to sauces and marinades without the harsh bite of fresh chiles. *Chipotles en adobo* are widely available in well-stocked supermarkets and Latino groceries.

LAMB CHOPS GRILLED IN ROSEMARY SMOKE

Slash the edges of the chops in 1 or 2 places to prevent curling.

To make the herb paste, in a small bowl, mix together the rosemary, garlic, salt, pepper, and the 2 teaspoons olive oil to make a thick paste. Add a little more olive oil if needed to achieve the desired consistency. Rub the meat all over with the paste. Let rest at room temperature for at least 15 minutes or up to 1 hour, or cover and refrigerate overnight. Bring to room temperature before grilling, if necessary.

Prepare a charcoal or gas grill for direct cooking over high heat (page 106). Put the rosemary stems on the charcoal or directly on the gas burners. (As the chops cook, the rosemary paste will char and fall off into the fire to provide even more rosemary smoke.) As the rosemary begins to smoke, arrange the chops over direct heat, and grill, covered, turning often, to the desired doneness, 3–6 minutes on each side. (Move the chops to a cooler area of the grill if flare-ups occur.) Test for doneness by inserting an instant-read thermometer away from the bone or by cutting into the chops near the bone. Remove the chops from the grill when the thermometer registers 130°F (54°C) and the meat is still quite pink near the bone for medium-rare.

Transfer the chops to a platter and let rest, tented loosely with aluminum foil, for 5 minutes. Serve 3 chops per diner, garnished with rosemary sprigs.

MAKES 4 SERVINGS

SMOKE AS FLAVORING

You can enhance the smoky flavor of grilled foods by using special hardwood coals or by adding hardwood chips or water-soaked woody herbs such as rosemary, thyme, or oregano to the charcoal, as is done in this recipe. Hardwood chips should be soaked in water for at least 30 minutes or up to 1 hour before using, and then placed directly on the coals in a covered grill. For gas grills, add chips to a smoker box or make a small packet of chips in aluminum foil, pierce the foil in a few spots, and place directly over the flame.

12 lamb loin chops, at least 1½ inches (4 cm) thick, trimmed of excess fat

FOR THE HERB PASTE:

¼ cup (⅓ oz/10 g) chopped fresh rosemary leaves or 2 tablespoons dried

8 cloves garlic, minced

2 teaspoons salt

1 teaspoon pepper

2 teaspoons olive oil, or more if needed

8 or more large rosemary stems with leaves, soaked in water for at least 30 minutes, plus sprigs for garnish

WINTER FARE

On blustery winter days, nothing could be better than savory braised lamb chops, thick rib steaks with winter vegetables, or a tender steak smothered in onions and peppers. Other stick-to-your-ribs dishes in this chapter include pork chops with sautéed apple and onion and veal chops simmered with paprika and sour cream—comfort food with a touch of sophistication.

CHICKEN-FRIED STEAKS WITH CREAM GRAVY

Pound the steaks lightly with a meat mallet to an even thickness of about ½ inch (12 mm). In a shallow bowl or deep plate, mix together the flour, paprika, thyme, sage, salt, black pepper, and cayenne. Set aside 1 tablespoon of the seasoned flour for the gravy. In another bowl, lightly beat the eggs with ½ cup (4 fl oz/ 125 ml) of the half-and-half. Dredge the steaks in the seasoned flour, then dip in the egg mixture, then dredge in the flour again. Let stand on a wire rack for at least 15 minutes or up to 30 minutes to set the coating.

Put an ovenproof platter lined with paper towels in the oven and preheat to 150°F (65°C). In a large, heavy frying pan over high heat, pour in the oil to a depth of ½ inch (12 mm) and heat until hot but not smoking. Add the steaks, in batches if necessary to avoid crowding, and fry until browned and crisp, 2–3 minutes on each side. Transfer the steaks to the platter in the oven while you make the gravy.

Pour off all but 1 tablespoon of the drippings from the pan. Over medium-high heat, stir in the 1 tablespoon reserved seasoned flour and stir with a wooden spoon to make a roux. Whisk in the remaining 1 cup (8 fl oz/250 ml) half-and-half and the stock. Add the Worcestershire sauce, Tabasco, and salt and pepper to taste. Cook for 3–4 minutes, whisking often. Add more stock if the gravy seems too thick. Strain the gravy through a fine-mesh sieve to remove any flecks of coating, if you wish. Taste and adjust the seasoning with salt and pepper.

Transfer the steaks to individual plates, spoon the gravy on top, and serve with the sweet potato biscuits, if desired.

MAKES 4 SERVINGS

PANFRYING TIPS

Panfrying is a great way to cook thin chops, cutlets, and steaks. You can create a crust using dried bread crumbs or flour, or season the meat with a spice rub or salt, pepper, and dried herbs. Be sure to use a large, heavy frying pan, which will distribute heat evenly, and don't crowd the meat while cooking or it will steam instead of fry. For best results, use a neutral-flavored oil with a high smoking point, such as peanut or corn oil. To make sure the oil is hot enough, dip one corner of the meat in the oil first and see if it sizzles.

4 thin beef sirloin or top round steaks, about ½ inch (12 mm) thick, trimmed of excess fat

1 cup (5 oz/155 g) all-purpose (plain) flour

1 teaspoon paprika

1 teaspoon dried thyme

1 teaspoon dried sage

1 teaspoon salt

1 teaspoon freshly ground black pepper

½ teaspoon cayenne pepper

2 eggs

1½ cups (12 fl oz/375 ml) half-and-half (half cream)

Corn or peanut oil for frying

½ cup (4 fl oz/125 ml) beef stock (page 110) or prepared broth, or more if needed

1 or 2 dashes of Worcestershire sauce

1 or 2 dashes of Tabasco or other hot sauce

Sweet potato biscuits for serving (page 111) (optional)

STEAK SMOTHERED IN ONIONS AND PEPPERS

FOR THE SPICE RUB:

1 tablespoon paprika

1½ teaspoons salt

1 teaspoon freshly ground
black pepper

1 teaspoon dried thyme

1 teaspoon chili powder

3 lb (1.5 kg) boneless
chuck or top round steak,
at least 1½ inches
(4 cm) thick, trimmed
of excess fat

2 tablespoons olive oil

½ cup (4 fl oz/125 ml)
dry red wine

2 yellow onions, sliced

3 cloves garlic, chopped

3 red or yellow bell
peppers (capsicums),
sliced

Smashed sweet potatoes
for serving (page 111)
(optional)

To make the rub, in a small bowl, combine the paprika, salt, black pepper, thyme, and chili powder. Rub the meat all over with the rub. Let stand at room temperature for at least 15 minutes or up to 1 hour, or cover and refrigerate overnight. Bring to room temperature, if necessary, before cooking.

Preheat the oven to 350°F (180°C).

In a large Dutch oven, heat the olive oil over medium-high heat. Add the meat and brown on all sides, about 7 minutes total. Transfer the meat to a platter and set aside.

Add the wine to the pan and deglaze the pan, scraping up any browned bits from the bottom. In a bowl, mix together the onions, garlic, and peppers. Return the meat to the pan. Cover the meat with the onion mixture and cover the pan. Transfer the pan to the oven and cook until the beef is tender, about 1½ hours.

Using a slotted spoon, transfer the meat to a serving platter and arrange the onion mixture on top. Skim the pan juices of any surface fat and spoon the juices over the vegetables and meat. Serve with a side of smashed sweet potatoes, if desired.

MAKES 4–6 SERVINGS

BELL PEPPERS

A member of the genus *Capsicum,* which also includes fiery chile peppers, the bell, or sweet, pepper is an American favorite. Green bell peppers were once the only kind widely available, but in recent years it has become easier to find the sweeter and more versatile red, yellow, orange, purple, and even dark brown peppers in supermarkets. Bell peppers can be eaten raw or cooked, peeled or unpeeled. They add color, flavor, and nutrients to salads, sauces, braises, and savory stews.

VEAL CHOPS PAPRIKASH

To make the rub, in a small bowl, mix together the salt, pepper, and the two paprikas. Slash the edges of the chops in 1 or 2 places to prevent curling. Sprinkle the chops all over with the rub. Let stand at room temperature for at least 15 minutes or up to 1 hour, or cover and refrigerate overnight. Bring to room temperature if necessary before cooking.

In a large, heavy frying pan over medium-high heat, heat the olive oil. Add the chops and brown for about 2 minutes on each side. Reduce the heat to medium and cover the pan. Cook until an instant-read thermometer inserted away from the bone registers 145°F (63°C) and the meat is lightly pink when cut into near the bone, 4–5 minutes longer. Transfer the chops to a serving platter and tent loosely with aluminum foil while you make the sauce.

Pour off all but 1 tablespoon of the drippings from the pan. Add the shallots, mushrooms, and the 1 teaspoon sweet paprika. Sauté over medium-high heat until the shallots are translucent, 3–4 minutes. Add the wine and deglaze the pan, scraping up any browned bits from the bottom. Cook for 1 minute longer, stirring often. Remove the pan from the heat and stir in the sour cream. Season to taste with salt and pepper.

Transfer the chops to individual plates, spoon the sauce on top, sprinkle with sweet paprika, and serve.

MAKES 4 SERVINGS

PAPRIKA
Derived from dried and ground red chiles, paprika is used for flavor and color in many cuisines, including Hungarian, Spanish, and Cajun. Paprika ranges from mild to hot, depending on the chiles used to make it. American paprika is often bland, but Hungarian paprika is full of flavor and can be found in mild (sweet) and hot versions. Spanish paprika is also flavorful and ranges from mild (sweet, or *dulce*) to medium-hot (bittersweet, or *agrodulce*) to hot *(picante)*. Paprika makes a great addition to spice rubs, especially for grilled meats.

FOR THE PAPRIKA RUB:

2 teaspoons salt

1 teaspoon freshly ground pepper

1 tablespoon sweet paprika

1½ teaspoons hot paprika

4 loin or rib veal chops, at least 1½ inches (4 cm) thick, trimmed of excess fat

2 tablespoons olive oil

3 shallots, chopped

3 oz (90 g) white mushrooms, brushed clean and chopped

1 teaspoon sweet paprika, plus more for garnish

1 cup (8 fl oz/250 ml) dry white wine

½ cup (4 oz/125 g) sour cream

Salt and freshly ground pepper

PORK CHOPS WITH APPLE AND ONION

4 center-cut pork loin
chops, at least 1½ inches
(4 cm) thick

FOR THE RUB:

1 tablespoon dried sage

2 teaspoons salt

½ teaspoon freshly
ground pepper

2 tablespoons olive oil

1 yellow onion, halved
and thinly sliced

1 green apple, quartered
and sliced

½ cup (4 fl oz/125 ml) dry
vermouth or white wine

Slash the edges of the chops in 1 or 2 places to prevent curling. To make the rub, in a small bowl combine the sage, salt, and pepper. Rub the pork chops all over with the rub. Let stand at room temperature for at least 15 minutes or up to 1 hour, or cover and refrigerate overnight. Bring to room temperature, if necessary, before cooking.

In a large frying pan over medium-high heat, heat the olive oil. Add the chops and brown for about 2 minutes on each side. Reduce the heat to medium and cover the pan. Cook until the meat is lightly pink near the bone or an instant-read thermometer inserted away from the bone registers 145°F (63°C), 4–5 minutes longer. Transfer the chops to a platter and tent them loosely with aluminum foil while you make the sauce.

Pour off all but 1 tablespoon of the drippings from the pan. Add the onion and apple and sauté until the onion is translucent, about 5 minutes. Add the vermouth and deglaze the pan, scraping up any browned bits from the bottom.

Spoon the apple and onion mixture onto individual plates. Place the pork chops on top, drizzle with the pan juices, and serve.

MAKES 4 SERVINGS

COOKING WITH APPLES
The sweet and tart flavor of apples is a delicious counterpoint to the rich taste of pork. Applesauce is the classic condiment for pork, but spiced apples, apple chutney, or—as in this recipe—sautéed apple slices are excellent alternatives. Tart varieties such as Granny Smith, pippin, or Fuji work best for cooking. Onion and vermouth add aroma and depth of flavor to the apple here, but shallots or red bell peppers and sherry, Port, or hard cider can produce equally tasty and nuanced dishes.

BRAISED LAMB SHOULDER CHOPS

Slash the edges of the chops in 1 or 2 places to prevent curling.

In a bowl, mix together the garlic powder, rosemary, dried oregano, salt, lemon pepper, ½ teaspoon cinnamon, and allspice. Rub the lamb all over with the rub. Let stand at room temperature for at least 15 minutes and up to 1 hour, or cover and refrigerate overnight. Bring to room temperature, if necessary, before cooking.

Preheat the oven to 350°F (180°C).

In a large, ovenproof sauté pan or casserole with cover, heat the olive oil over medium-high heat. Add the chops, in batches if necessary to avoid crowding, and sear, 3–4 minutes on each side. Transfer the browned chops to a platter. Add the garlic, fresh oregano, and chopped mint to the pan and sauté until the garlic is softened, 3–4 minutes. Add the wine and tomato and stir to mix. Return all the chops to the pan, in layers if necessary to fit. Cover the pan and braise in the oven until the lamb is very tender, about 1 hour. Using tongs or a slotted spoon, transfer the chops to a platter and keep warm. Skim any fat from the surface of the sauce and stir in the tomato paste and ½ teaspoon cinnamon. Taste and adjust the seasoning. Place over medium heat and cook, stirring often, until thickened, about 5 minutes.

Arrange the chops on individual plates. Spoon the sauce over the chops and garnish with the mint sprigs.

Serving Tip: This dish goes perfectly with Mint Pilaf (page 111).

Note: To peel tomatoes, score an X at the blossom end and plunge them into boiling water for 15–30 seconds. Remove, run under cold water to stop the cooking, and peel from the X. To seed, slice them in half crosswise and squeeze out the seeds.

MAKES 4 SERVINGS

LAMB CUTS

Almost any cut of lamb is tender enough to grill, broil, or sauté; only the comparatively tough shanks need long, slow cooking, such as braising, for best results. Lamb loin and rib chops, just like tender beef steaks, come from the back and rib area of the animal. The shoulder, used in this recipe, is more muscular and is therefore chewier—but very flavorful. Tender lamb chops are best served rare or medium-rare, whereas the tougher shoulder chops taste better cooked to medium or well done.

8 lamb shoulder chops, trimmed of excess fat

FOR THE HERB RUB:

2 tablespoons garlic powder

1 tablespoon *each* dried rosemary and oregano

2 teaspoons salt

1 teaspoon lemon pepper (page 98)

½ teaspoon ground cinnamon

¼ teaspoon ground allspice

2 tablespoons olive oil

6 cloves garlic, chopped

2 tablespoons *each* chopped fresh oregano and chopped fresh mint, plus fresh mint sprigs for garnish

1 cup (8 fl oz/250 ml) dry red wine

1 large tomato, peeled, seeded, and diced (see Note)

2 tablespoons tomato paste

½ teaspoon ground cinnamon

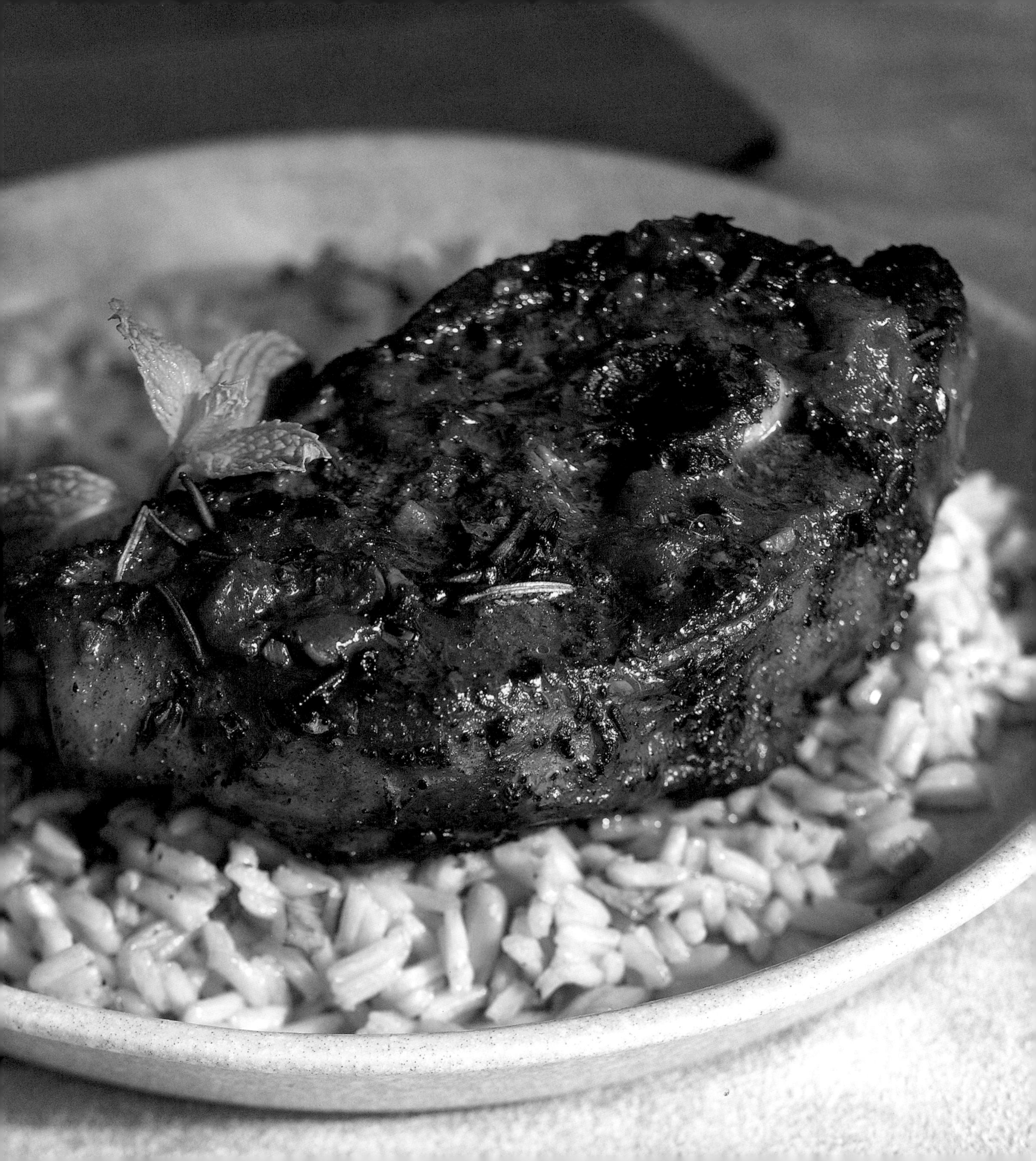

ARGENTINE-STYLE STUFFED FLANK STEAK

One thick 1½ lb (750 g) flank steak, trimmed of excess fat and silver skin

1 tablespoon *each* red wine vinegar and paprika

2 tablespoons tomato paste

2 cloves garlic, minced

4 tablespoons olive oil

¼ lb (125 g) prosciutto, thinly sliced

1 bunch spinach, carefully washed and stemmed

1 carrot, peeled and grated

½ yellow onion, sliced

1 red bell pepper (capsicum), roasted (page 65) peeled, and sliced

1 cup (1 oz/30 g) fresh basil leaves

½ cup (2 oz/60 g) *each* dried bread crumbs and grated pecorino romano cheese

2 teaspoons dried thyme

Salt and ground pepper

½ cup (4 fl oz/125 ml) *each* white wine and Marsala

1 cup (8 fl oz/250 ml) beef stock (page 110)

1 tablespoon Worcestershire sauce

Butterfly the meat by slicing horizontally, stopping about ¾ inch (2 cm) from the other side. Open up the meat and pound with a meat mallet to an even thickness of ½ inch (12 mm).

Preheat the oven to 350°F (180°C). Mix together the vinegar, paprika, 1 tablespoon of the tomato paste, garlic, and 1 table-spoon of the olive oil. Stir to form a thick paste. Smear the paste on the open side of the steak, reserving 1 tablespoon. Layer the prosciutto, spinach, carrot, onion, bell pepper, and basil on top. In a small bowl, combine the bread crumbs, cheese, 1 teaspoon of the thyme, and salt and pepper to taste; sprinkle the mixture on top. Roll the meat from the long end into a tight cylinder and tie with kitchen string (page 97). Turn it seam side down and rub with 1 tablespoon of the olive oil. Sprinkle with salt and pepper and the remaining 1 teaspoon thyme.

In a large, heavy frying pan over medium-high heat, heat the remaining 2 tablespoons olive oil. Add the meat and brown on all sides, about 5 minutes. Transfer to a flameproof roasting pan, seam side down, and roast for about 45 minutes. Lift the meat and pour the white wine into the pan underneath to keep the meat from sticking. Roast until an instant-read thermometer inserted in the center registers 130°F (54°C), about 1 hour. Transfer to a board and tent loosely with aluminum foil.

Add the Marsala to the roasting pan and place over high heat. Scrape up any browned bits from the bottom of the pan. Whisk in the stock, Worcestershire sauce, and the remaining 1 tablespoon tomato paste and cook, stirring often, until reduced by half, about 5 minutes. Strain the sauce through a fine-mesh sieve.

To serve, remove the string from the meat and slice it thickly into rounds. Transfer to individual plates and ladle the sauce over.

MAKES 4–6 SERVINGS

MATAMBRE

The inspiration for this stuffed flank steak is *Matambre,* a favorite dish of Argentina, where beef is the soul of the cuisine. *Matambre* means "kill hunger" in Spanish, and legend has it that early travelers across the *pampas* (grasslands) took the dish with them to kill their hunger on their journeys. *Matambre* is often served sliced as an appetizer, but it also makes a dramatic main course. Try it with a serving of Fried Polenta (page 110).

RIB STEAK WITH WINTER VEGETABLES AND ZINFANDEL GRAVY

Place the beef in a nonreactive baking dish. Using a small, sharp knife, make slits over the surface of the meat. Insert the garlic slices into the slits. Sprinkle the meat all over with salt and pepper and 2 tablespoons of the thyme, and set aside at room temperature for at least 15 minutes or up to 1 hour.

Preheat the oven to 400°F (200°C). Peel and quarter the potatoes and onions. In a large bowl, combine the carrots, turnips, potatoes, onions, and whole garlic cloves. Drizzle with 1 tablespoon of the olive oil and sprinkle with salt and pepper and the remaining 1½ teaspoons thyme. Arrange the vegetables in a single layer on a baking sheet and roast, stirring often, until tender, 35–40 minutes. Remove from the oven and set aside.

About 10 minutes before the vegetables are done, coat the bottom of a large, ovenproof pan with the remaining 1 tablespoon olive oil. Add the meat to the pan and sear over medium-high heat for 4–5 minutes on each side. Transfer to the oven and roast to the desired doneness. Remove from the heat when still red at the center for rare (120°F/49°C), or when deep pink at the center for medium-rare (130°F/54°C). Let the meat rest, tented loosely with aluminum foil, for 10 minutes before serving.

To make the gravy, pour off all but 1 tablespoon of the drippings from the roasting pan. Heat over medium heat and whisk in the flour. Whisk in the wine, beef stock, tomato paste, Worcestershire, soy sauce, and Tabasco. Cook, stirring often, until the mixture is thickened, 5–6 minutes. Season to taste with salt and pepper.

Arrange the steak on a platter surrounded by the roasted vegetables. Spoon the gravy over the meat and serve.

MAKES 4 SERVINGS

SEASONAL VEGETABLES

One principle of the American food revolution is to cook with what's in season. Winter is the time for acorn squash baked with butter and maple syrup, beets steamed with their own greens and balsamic vinegar, and, as we see in this recipe, roots and tubers such as carrots, turnips, and potatoes roasted with garlic, onions, and thyme.

1 piece prime rib, 2–3 lb (1–1.5 kg), 2 bones thick

8 cloves garlic, 4 thinly sliced and 4 whole

Salt and freshly ground pepper

2 tablespoons plus 1½ teaspoons chopped fresh thyme

2 small potatoes

2 large yellow onions

2 *each* carrots and turnips, peeled and cut into 1-inch (2.5-cm) chunks

2 tablespoons olive oil

FOR THE GRAVY:

1 tablespoon all-purpose (plain) flour

½ cup (4 fl oz/125 ml) Zinfandel or other full-bodied red wine

1 cup (8 fl oz/250 ml) beef stock (page 110)

2 tablespoons tomato paste

1 teaspoon *each* Worcestershire sauce, soy sauce, and Tabasco

Salt and freshly ground pepper

HOLIDAY FEASTS

For a dramatic presentation and delicious meal, nothing can surpass a whole roast, carved at the table. Traditional favorites include standing prime rib roast with a spicy crust or crown roast of pork stuffed with baby vegetables. And a succulent roast beef tenderloin flavored with mushrooms or veal cooked Provençal style will make any occasion feel special.

STANDING PRIME RIB ROAST WITH HORSERADISH CRUST
90

CROWN ROAST OF PORK WITH BABY VEGETABLE STUFFING
93

RACK OF LAMB WITH MUSTARD–BREAD CRUMB CRUST
94

ROAST BEEF TENDERLOIN
WITH MUSHROOM-MADEIRA STUFFING
97

VEAL PROVENÇALE WITH ROASTED TOMATOES
98

TUSCAN-STYLE ROAST LOIN OF PORK
101

STANDING PRIME RIB ROAST WITH HORSERADISH CRUST

To make the crust, in a small bowl, mix together the mustard, ¼ cup horseradish, bread crumbs, rosemary, garlic, salt, and pepper. Rub the mixture all over the meat and let stand at room temperature for at least 15 minutes or up to 1 hour, or cover and refrigerate overnight. Bring to room temperature, if necessary, before cooking.

Preheat the oven to 350°F (180°C). Oil a roasting pan just large enough to hold the roast. Place the rib roast, fat side up, in the pan and roast until nicely browned, about 1 hour. Check for doneness by inserting an instant-read thermometer away from the bone or by cutting into the meat near the bone. For rare beef, remove the roast at 120°–125°F (49°–52°C) or when the meat is red near the bone; for medium-rare, remove at 130°F (54°C), when the meat is deep pink near the bone. Transfer the roast to a carving board and let rest, tented loosely with aluminum foil, for 10–12 minutes before serving.

Whisk ½ cup horseradish and the sour cream together in a small bowl. Carve the roast *(left)* into thick or thin slices as desired, transfer to individual plates, and serve with the horseradish sauce on top.

Variation Tip: If you prefer, you can also cook the rib roast on a grill. Prepare a charcoal or gas grill for indirect grilling over medium-high heat (page 106). Place the prepared roast, fat side up, over the cooler portion of the grill with a drip pan underneath and roast, covered, for 1 hour. Check for doneness as directed above.

MAKES 8–10 SERVINGS

CARVING RIB ROASTS

Carving prime rib, bone-in pork loin, and racks of lamb is easy when you have the butcher remove the chine bone that runs along the bottom of the roast. To carve, place the roast on a carving board; holding the knife parallel to the ribs, slice along the edge of the ribs, under the rib-eye, the meaty portion, to separate it from the bones, then slice the rib-eye as thinly or as thickly as you like. Or, you can cut between the bones for bone-in slices.

FOR THE CRUST:

½ cup (4 oz/125 g) Dijon mustard

¼ cup (2 oz/60 g) prepared horseradish

¾ cup (3 oz/90 g) dried bread crumbs

2 tablespoons chopped fresh rosemary or 1 tablespoon dried

6 cloves garlic, minced

2 teaspoons salt

2 teaspoons freshly ground pepper

1 standing prime rib roast (4 ribs), 6–8 lb (3–4 kg), chine bone removed by the butcher

½ cup (4 oz/125 g) prepared horseradish

½ cup (4 oz/125 g) sour cream

CROWN ROAST OF PORK
WITH BABY VEGETABLE STUFFING

FOR THE SAGE RUB:

2 tablespoons chopped
fresh sage

1 tablespoon garlic powder

1 tablespoon onion
powder

2 teaspoons salt

1 tablespoon freshly
ground pepper

1 crown roast of pork
(16 ribs), about 8 lb (4 kg),
chine bone removed by
the butcher

12 young, tender carrots,
trimmed if desired

12 baby turnips, trimmed
if desired

12 very small new
potatoes or 6 small
potatoes, halved

2 tablespoons olive oil

12 fresh white button
or cremini mushrooms

12 pearl onions, blanched
and peeled *(far right)*

Salt and freshly ground
pepper

To make the rub, in a small bowl, mix together the sage, garlic powder, onion powder, salt, and pepper. Sprinkle the rub all over the pork, reserving 2 tablespoons for the vegetable stuffing. Let stand at room temperature for at least 15 minutes or up to 1 hour.

Preheat the oven to 350°F (180°C). Oil a roasting pan just large enough to hold the pork. Place the crown roast bone side down in the pan and roast until nicely browned, about 1 hour. Check for doneness by inserting an instant-read thermometer away from the bone or by cutting into the meat near the bone. The pork is done when the internal temperature is 150°F (65°C); remove it from the heat just before it is done, when the meat is still pink near the bone and the temperature is about 145°F (63°C). Transfer to a carving board, still bone side down, and let rest, tented loosely with aluminum foil, for about 10 minutes before serving. (The meat will continue to cook as it rests)

In a saucepan, combine the carrots, turnips, and potatoes with lightly salted water to cover. Bring to a boil over high heat, then reduce the heat to medium and cook until the vegetables are still firm but can be pierced with the tip of a sharp knife, 5–6 minutes. Drain and set aside.

Meanwhile, in a large saucepan over medium-high heat, heat the olive oil. Add the mushrooms, peeled pearl onions, and the parboiled vegetables and sauté until the vegetables are tender, 4–5 minutes. Sprinkle with the reserved 2 tablespoons rub and season to taste with salt and pepper.

To serve, turn the crown roast so that the bones point up. Fill the crown with the vegetable mixture. At the table, slice between the chops and arrange on individual plates with the vegetables.

MAKES 8–10 SERVINGS

PEELING PEARL
ONIONS

Small onions, also called pearl or baby onions, can be difficult to peel. To ease the process, put unpeeled pearl onions in a saucepan with boiling water to cover. Blanch for 1 minute, drain, and cool under running cold water. Cut off the ends and peel with a small, sharp knife. The skin should slip off easily.

RACK OF LAMB WITH
MUSTARD–BREAD CRUMB CRUST

Season the lamb generously with salt and pepper. Let the meat stand at room temperature for at least 15 minutes or up to 1 hour before cooking.

Preheat the oven to 450°F (230°C).

In a large, ovenproof frying pan over medium-high heat, heat the olive oil. When the oil starts to smoke, add the racks, fat side down. Sear until golden brown on all sides, about 2 minutes on each side. (Do not crowd the pan; use 2 frying pans if necessary.) When the racks are browned, transfer them to a platter and set aside to cool. Reserve the pan(s).

To make the crust, in a bowl, combine the bread crumbs, rosemary, and garlic powder and mix well. Add olive oil until the bread crumbs have the feel of wet sand; you may need more or less than ¼ cup. Using a spatula, spread the mustard over the meat of each rack of lamb, excluding the bones. Then pack the bread crumb mixture over the mustard, which will help it adhere.

Return the racks to the pan(s) and roast in the oven until an instant-read thermometer inserted away from the bone registers 130°F (54°C) and the meat is quite pink when cut into near the bone for medium-rare, 12–15 minutes. Transfer to a carving board and let rest, loosely tented with aluminum foil, for 5–10 minutes before serving.

Carve into chops and serve 2 to each diner.

MAKES 4–6 SERVINGS

PAN-ROASTING

Pan-roasting is an easy chef's trick that involves browning meat on the stove top and then finishing it by roasting in a hot oven. In a restaurant this method allows the chef to precook the meat, and then ready it quickly with a brief final roasting. For home cooks, the technique offers the convenience of partially cooking the roast ahead of time, while also ensuring a delicious and nicely browned surface and perfectly cooked interior. For more on roasting, see page 109.

2 racks of lamb, about 1½ lb (750 g) each, frenched by the butcher

Salt and freshly ground pepper

1 tablespoon olive oil

FOR THE CRUST:

½ cup (2 oz/60 g) dried bread crumbs

2 teaspoons finely chopped fresh rosemary

2 teaspoons garlic powder or granulated garlic

¼ cup (2 fl oz/60 ml) olive oil, or as needed

2 tablespoons Dijon mustard

ROAST BEEF TENDERLOIN
WITH MUSHROOM-MADEIRA STUFFING

FOR THE STUFFING:

1 tablespoon *each* unsalted butter and olive oil

1 lb (500 g) white mushrooms, chopped

6 cloves garlic, chopped

¼ cup (2 fl oz/60 ml) dry Madeira or sherry

½ cup (¾ oz/20 g) chopped fresh flat-leaf (Italian) parsley

1 cup (2 oz/60 g) fresh bread crumbs

Salt and ground pepper

4–5 lb (2–2.5 kg) beef tenderloin (fillet)

Salt and ground pepper

1 tablespoon olive oil

1 tablespoon unsalted butter

1 tablespoon all-purpose (plain) flour

1 cup (8 fl oz/250 ml) beef stock (page 110)

¼ cup (2 fl oz/60 ml) dry Madeira or sherry

1 tablespoon tomato paste

Dash of Worcestershire sauce

Preheat the oven to 400°F (200°C). To make the stuffing, in a frying pan over medium heat, melt the butter with the olive oil. Add the mushrooms and garlic and sauté, stirring often until softened, about 5 minutes. Stir in the Madeira, parsley, and bread crumbs to make a thick, moist paste. Remove from the heat, season to taste with salt and pepper, and set aside to cool.

Butterfly the roast by cutting down the center lengthwise, stopping about ¾ inch (2 cm) from the other side. Open it up and pound it with a meat mallet to an even thickness of ¾ inch. Sprinkle with salt and pepper.

When the stuffing has cooled slightly, spread it evenly on the cut side of the meat. Roll the meat into a cylinder and tie with kitchen string *(right)*. In a heavy, ovenproof frying pan over high heat, heat the olive oil until smoking. Add the rolled roast and sear, turning often, for 6–7 minutes. Transfer the pan to the oven and roast to the desired doneness, about 10 minutes. Test for doneness using an instant-read thermometer or by cutting into the meat. For rare beef, remove the roast at 120°–125°F (49°–52°C) or when red at the center; for medium rare, remove at 130°F (54°C) or when deep pink at the center. Transfer to a board and let rest, tented with aluminum foil, for 5 minutes before serving.

In the same pan, melt the butter over medium heat. Stir in the flour, and whisk in the stock, the Madeira, tomato paste, and Worcestershire sauce. Cook, whisking, until the sauce is thickened, about 5 minutes. Season with salt and pepper. Remove the strings from the roast and slice it into thick rounds. Arrange the slices on individual plates, spoon the sauce over, and serve at once.

MAKES 8 SERVINGS

TYING A ROAST

Place the meat on a platter or cutting board, cut side up. Season the meat and add any stuffing, if using. Cut several lengths of kitchen string about one-third again as long as the thickness of the piece of meat. Use at least three strings for each roast; for larger cuts use more strings. Put the strings underneath the meat, leaving equal lengths on either side. Draw the strings up around the roast and tie them off. Cut away excess string. Remove and discard the strings before carving the roast.

VEAL PROVENÇALE WITH ROASTED TOMATOES

To make the rub, in a small bowl, mix together the herbes de Provence, paprika, garlic powder, orange zest, salt, and lemon pepper. Score the top of the veal roast in 2 or 3 places. Rub the meat all over with the 1 tablespoon olive oil. Rub the meat all over with the rub, reserving 1 tablespoon. Let stand at room temperature for at least 15 minutes or up to 1 hour before cooking.

Preheat the oven to 375°F (190°C). Oil a roasting pan just large enough to hold the veal.

Place the veal roast fat side up in the pan and roast until nicely browned on the outside, 40–45 minutes. Veal is done when the internal temperature reaches 145°–150°F (63°–65°C) with lightly pink and very juicy meat. Test for doneness by inserting an instant-read thermometer away from the bone or by cutting into the meat near the bone. Remove the roast from the heat just before it is done (140°F/60°C) and let it rest, tented loosely with aluminum foil, for 5–10 minutes before serving. (The roast will continue cooking while it rests.) Leave the oven on.

Core the tomatoes deeply by running a small, sharp knife into the stem end and around the core. Place 1 teaspoon of the chopped garlic and 2 olives in the space left by the core of each tomato. Drizzle with olive oil and sprinkle with the reserved 1 tablespoon herb rub. Place the tomatoes in an oiled roasting pan, cored side up, and roast until softened and heated through, 10–12 minutes.

To serve, cut the roast into chops or thick slices, spoon the pan juices over, and serve with the roasted tomatoes.

MAKES 6–8 SERVINGS

LEMON PEPPER
A blend of coarsely ground black pepper and dried lemon peel, lemon pepper is available in most markets. Some spice companies offer blends that also include cumin, red pepper, oregano, thyme, dried onion and garlic, or paprika. You can make your own lemon pepper by mixing coarsely ground pepper with an equal amount of dried lemon zest coarsely ground in a food processor. Use lemon pepper in spice and herb rubs; on pork, lamb, chicken, or fish; or whenever you want the bite of pepper with an underlying lemony flavor.

FOR THE RUB:

2 tablespoons herbes de Provence

2 tablespoons paprika

2 tablespoons garlic powder

1½ teaspoons grated orange zest

1½ teaspoons salt

1 teaspoon lemon pepper *(far left)*

1 boneless veal loin roast, about 5 lb (2.5 kg), or bone-in, chine bone removed by the butcher

1 tablespoon olive oil, plus more for drizzling

4 large tomatoes

4 teaspoons chopped garlic

8 pitted black olives such as kalamata

TUSCAN-STYLE ROAST LOIN OF PORK

FOR THE HERB PASTE:

2 tablespoons chopped fresh thyme or 1 tablespoon dried

1 tablespoon chopped fresh sage, or 1½ teaspoons dried

6 cloves garlic, minced

2 teaspoons salt

1 teaspoon freshly ground pepper

2 tablespoons olive oil, or as needed

1 boneless pork loin roast, 4–6 lb (2–3 kg), or bone-in with the chine bone removed, trimmed of excess fat

Preheat the oven to 350°F (180°C).

To make the paste, in a small bowl, mix together the thyme, sage, garlic, salt, pepper, and enough olive oil to make a thick paste; you may need more or less than 2 tablespoons.

Score the top of the roast in 1 or 2 places. Rub the herb paste all over the meat and let stand at room temperature for at least 15 minutes or up to 1 hour before cooking, or cover and refrigerate overnight. Bring the roast to room temperature, if necessary, before cooking.

Oil a roasting pan just large enough to hold the pork. Place the pork in the pan, fat-side up, and roast for 45 minutes, or longer if needed. Test for doneness using an instant-read thermometer or by cutting into the meat. Loin of pork should be removed from the heat when the internal temperature reaches 145°F (63°C) or when the meat is slightly pink at the center. Let rest, tented loosely with aluminum foil, for 10 minutes, slice, and serve.

MAKES 6–8 SERVINGS

ARISTA

Tuscan-style roast pork is known as *arista*, a name that probably comes from *aristos*, the Greek word for "best." The implication is that the loin is the best part of the pig and roasting is the best way to cook it. *Arista* is traditionally cooked on a spit. To do this yourself, set up a rotisserie according to the manufacturer's directions in a charcoal or gas grill and prepare for indirect grilling over medium-high heat (page 106). Center the roast on the spit and roast for 45 minutes or longer if needed. Test for doneness as directed for oven roasting *(above)*.

STEAK AND CHOP BASICS

Steaks and chops, small pieces of tender meat that can be cooked quickly over a hot fire, have been favorite cuts since the beginning of cookery. When early hunter-gatherers cooked their meat, they didn't have stoves and ovens or even pots. They cut tender meat into serving-sized pieces and skewered them on sticks held near the fire or ran sharpened branches through larger chunks to spit-roast over burning coals. The appeal of grilling and roasting tender meat over high heat is that the surface browns to make a savory crust while the inside of the meat stays tender and juicy. What's more, cooking steaks and chops is easy and doesn't usually involve long preparation times.

ABOUT STEAKS AND CHOPS

Steaks and chops are basically the same cuts from different animals. Pieces of tender meat, with or without bones, cut from steer carcasses (and any large animal such as deer, elk, or moose) are referred to as steaks. The same cuts from the loin, sirloin, and rib areas of smaller animals such as pigs, lambs, or calves are referred to as chops. Both kinds are cut from the back and ribs, areas of the animal that get less exercise than the legs, hips, and shoulders and thus yield tender meat.

Most steaks and chops need only be seasoned and then cooked briefly over a hot grill or in the oven to make a delicious meal. Tougher muscles from other areas must be cooked longer to become tender.

BEEF

If you order a steak in an American restaurant or steak house, you'll be served a piece of tender beef, most likely from the short loin (back) or rib area of the steer. Usually it comes grilled or broiled and served plain with a pat of butter or a bottled steak sauce, but occasionally it will come sautéed and served with a pan sauce, typically based on mushrooms.

A French chef will almost always sauté a steak and will often serve it with an elaborate sauce based on wine, butter, or cream. The most famous Italian steak is the *bistecca fiorentina* (page 58), a thick porterhouse rubbed with olive oil and grilled over hardwood coals.

Steak is most flavorful when served rare (120°–125°F/49°–52°C) or medium-rare (130°–135°F/54°–57°C), although some prefer steaks that are cooked medium or well-done (140°–155°F/60°–68°C), a treatment that reduces tenderness but can still be flavorful.

The porterhouse and the T-bone, two of the most popular steaks in America, are both cut from the loin or back area and include a piece of the tenderloin and the larger loin muscle. Fillet steaks are cut from the tenderloin or fillet muscle that runs along the backbone; New York strip and other top-loin steaks are cut from the larger, but still tender, loin muscle.

Porterhouse and T-bone steaks are always sold bone-in; filet mignon, tournedos, chateaubriand, and other fillet steaks are always boneless. Variously named top-loin steaks (New York, Kansas City, strip, shell, top loin, club steaks) are sold either bone-in or boneless. Rib steaks are popular with American cooks. They are sold bone-in as rib steaks or boneless as rib-eye, Delmonico, market, or Spencer steaks.

Steaks cut from other areas of the steer are slightly chewier and often marinated before cooking. These include the flank steak from the belly area, the skirt and hanger steaks from the diaphragm, the chuck steak cut from the shoulder, and the culotte steak or tri-tip from the bottom sirloin. Larger pieces from tender areas of the steer such as fillet roast, prime rib, sirloin roast, or tri-tip can be roasted in an oven or a covered grill, or can be roasted on a spit.

PORK

Chops are the most popular cut of pork in America, but recent trends have made pork chops more difficult to cook successfully. Leaner pigs bred for today's fat-conscious eaters often yield tough, dried-out chops. Care must be taken not to overcook lean and tender pork, especially from the loin area. (Trichina parasites, are killed at 138°F/59°C, so pork need only be cooked to 145°F/63°C for safety.)

Chops are cut from the tender back or loin area of the pig, from the ribs and sirloin, and from the shoulder. Loin chops are often sold with a piece of tenderloin attached (much like a small porterhouse steak), but are also cut only from the loin and sold bone-in or boneless. Rib chops are also quite tender, although usually with a bit more fat. They are always sold bone-in. Chops cut from the sirloin (hip) and shoulder regions have more fat and connective tissue

and are chewier than the loin or rib chops. They should be cooked a little longer, to 155°–160°F (68°–71°C) for maximum flavor and tenderness.

Pork loin is also sold in larger pieces, both bone-in and boneless, to be roasted and then carved into chops or sliced. One popular and dramatic way to cook pork loin is a crown roast of pork, a bone-in pork loin tied in a circle and often stuffed before serving (page 93).

Pork tenderloin, the thin and very tender muscle that runs along the pig's backbone, is an increasingly popular cut. The small tenderloin (1–2 lb/500 g–1 kg), equivalent to beef tenderloin or fillet, is virtually without fat and is sold boneless and whole (often in packages of two tenderloins). Pork tenderloin can be roasted whole or cut into two pieces to make small, individual roasts. It can also be butterflied and grilled or sautéed. When sliced into medallions, it is even more versatile.

LAMB

The meat from young lamb has always been considered a delicacy. Roasted whole at village festivals or skewered and grilled over an open fire, lamb has been the preferred meat of Near Eastern and Asian cooks for thousands of years. When

cut into chops and grilled or pan-broiled, lamb is quick, easy to cook, and delicious to eat.

The most tender chops are cut from the loin or back. These usually include a piece of the tenderloin and the loin and resemble beef porterhouse steaks, but on a much smaller scale. Rib chops resemble beef rib steaks and include a bit more fat than loin chops, but have even more flavor.

Both loin and rib lamb chops are best grilled, broiled, or pan-broiled over medium-high heat to the medium-rare stage (130°–135°F/54°–57°C). A double-cut loin chop is extra thick (more than 1 inch/2.5 cm); a double-cut rib chop will include two rib bones. Cook these as you would a thick steak (page 22). Chops cut from the lamb shoulder and sirloin have more fat and connective tissue and are best when broiled to medium (140°F/60°C) or braised.

Rack of lamb is a set of ribs left whole and roasted; the ribs are then carved and served. One rack of seven or eight ribs will weigh 1–1½ lb (500–750 g) and will serve two people. Rib chops and racks of lamb are often frenched, a preparation in which the meat and fat is cut off the ends of the bones. Lamb from the United States, New Zealand, and Australia can be found in most markets.

VEAL

Veal is meat from calves, usually about four months old. Milk-fed veal is from calves fed only on milk or on special milk-based formulas; it is quite pale in color and very tender, and it has a light and subtle flavor. Range-fed or grass-fed veal is also from young animals, but these have been allowed to graze and develop meat with a light red color, a denser texture, and more robust flavor than milk-fed veal.

There has been controversy in recent years about the poor conditions in which some veal calves are raised. Some consumers prefer to purchase range-fed or "red" veal, since the animals will have been raised outdoors under "natural" conditions. Many also prefer the more intense flavor of the range-fed meat, while others find the mild and delicate character of milk-fed veal more appealing.

Chops and cutlets, also called scallops or scaloppine, are the most popular cuts of veal. They are virtually the same, except cutlets are boneless. Chops cut from the loin or back resemble slightly smaller and paler porterhouse steaks. Rib chops are almost as tender as loin chops and have a richer, more intense flavor. Chops cut from the shoulder and sirloin are also delicious, although with more fat and connective tissue.

Loin or rib chops should be cooked to medium-rare (135°F/57°C) or medium (145°F/63°C); shoulder and sirloin chops should be cooked to medium to medium-well (150°F/65°C) or braised. Veal cutlets or scallops are thin, tender slices of veal cut from the loin or leg. They are best sautéed or panfried and are often breaded before cooking.

TRIMMING AND CARVING

Before cooking steaks and chops, check them for large pieces of fat and trim it away. The fat is flavorful and protects the meat from drying out, and therefore should not be removed entirely, but too much rendered fat remaining in a pan after cooking can mar the texture of a sauce or gravy. A good rule of thumb is to trim the fat to a thin layer about ⅛ inch thick.

Some cooks prefer to remove the silver skin, also called the "fell," a thin layer of connective tissue, from pork loin, spareribs, steaks, and other cuts. This will improve the appearance as well as the tenderness of the meat.

Because most chops and small steaks are already a good size for serving, they require little in the way of carving skills. A sharp carving knife or boning knife, a large fork, and a platter or carving board are all the equipment needed for carving or preparing steaks and chops. A porterhouse or T-bone steak more than 2 inches (5 cm) thick can be carved at the table. First separate the fillet portion and the loin portion from the bone by running a sharp boning knife or small carving knife along either side of the central bone. Slice the fillet and the loin into ½-inch (12-mm) pieces and serve slices of both to each diner.

Thick boneless steaks such as chateaubriand should be sliced into ½-inch pieces at the table as well. For racks of lamb and bone-in roasts of beef, pork, or veal, have the butcher remove the chine bone; after cooking, just slice between the ribs to serve. Flank steaks and skirt steaks should be cut across the grain on the diagonal into thin slices for serving.

To butterfly a piece of beef or pork tenderloin, a flank steak, or a boneless leg of lamb, hold your knife parallel to the cutting board and make a horizontal cut most of the way through the meat, slicing almost through to the other side but leaving ½–1 inch (12 mm–2.5 cm) of meat uncut. Once you open and flatten the meat, using a meat mallet or rolling pin, you can then stuff or grill it.

COOKING METHODS
FOR STEAKS AND CHOPS

Here are tips on the most popular ways to prepare steaks and chops.

GRILLING AND BROILING

Grilling and broiling are favorite methods for cooking steaks and chops. Cooked this way at medium-high to high heat, the meat will reach the desired temperature in a short time while retaining maximum flavor.

Charcoal briquettes, often mixed with hardwoods, provide even cooking; mesquite, hickory, and oak will cook food more quickly and provide added flavor and intense, but often uneven, levels of heat.

Techniques for grilling and broiling are essentially the same: Clean and oil the grill or broiling pan. Pre-heat the broiler (grill) or gas grill to medium-high or high, or prepare a charcoal grill for high-heat grilling.

When grilling, it is best to build a three-level fire: One area should have high heat, one medium-high to medium heat, and one area should have no heat source under the grill. To build a charcoal fire, ignite the charcoal using a chimney starter, electric starter, or lighter fluid (the least appealing choice). Using a small ash shovel, trowel, or tongs, pile up about two-thirds of the coals under

one area of the grill, one-third under another, and leave one-third of the grill without any heat source. For hardwood coals, light the wood and burn it down to coals, and arrange as described above. For a gas grill, turn one burner to high, another to medium, and leave one burner off.

First, sear steaks or chops on high to medium-high heat, then move them to the medium area or the unheated area to continue cooking, covered, until done. If flare-ups occur while searing, move the meat to a cooler area of the grill. Do not use spray bottles to control flare-ups; in most cases they just wash off flavors, and may make the problem worse by causing fat to drip onto the flames.

SAUTÉING AND MAKING
A PAN SAUCE

Sautéing is a good way to cook small steaks and chops that are tender and low in fat such as tournedos and filet mignon, pork and veal cutlets, and boneless pork chops.

Sauter in French means "to jump," and the technique involves keeping ingredients moving in a small pan so that they cook quickly and do not stick. Usually the pan is left uncovered, but for larger chops, the pan can be covered to help the meat cook all the way through.

To sauté steaks and chops, heat a large, heavy frying pan or sauté pan over medium-high heat, add 1–2 tablespoons of olive oil or other vegetable oil, and brown the meat on both sides. Do not crowd the pan; sauté in batches, if necessary.

When sautéing thicker cuts of meat, first brown the outside, then reduce the heat to medium, and cook, covered, until the meat is cooked through. Transfer the food to a platter in a low oven while you make a pan sauce. Basic steps for making a pan sauce are shown, opposite.

1 Sautéing: Sauté garlic, shallots, onions, herbs, and other seasonings in the juices left in the pan used to cook the meat. Add more oil or butter, if needed.

2 Deglazing: Deglaze the pan with wine, cider, stock, or other liquid over high heat, stirring to scrape up any browned bits from the bottom of the pan. Bring to a boil, reduce the heat, and cook the liquid until reduced by half, or until thick and glossy.

3 Adding flavor: Stir in tomato paste, Worcestershire sauce, balsamic vinegar, hot-pepper sauce, or other seasonings as desired. Season to taste with salt and freshly ground pepper.

4 Thickening the sauce: If you like a thicker sauce, stir in 1 tablespoon cornstarch (cornflour) combined with 2 tablespoons of wine, water, or other liquid; or finish the sauce with butter, cream, or sour cream for a smooth texture and mellow flavor.

PANFRYING

Panfrying is an excellent method for cooking thin chops, cutlets, or steaks. For a crisp exterior, first bread the meat with seasoned flour, bread crumbs, crushed crackers, egg, milk, and/or other ingredients.

Peanut oil is the best oil for frying because of its high smoke point, although corn or other vegetable oils also work well. Olive oil has a lower smoke point than other oils, but you can still use it to panfry if you prefer the flavor. Breading will keep the meat from toughening and drying out in the hot oil and provides a pleasantly crunchy and savory crust.

To panfry steaks and chops, in a large, heavy frying pan over high heat, heat ½ inch (12 mm) oil. Fry the breaded chops, cutlets, or steaks, turning once, until the crust is browned on both sides. Do not crowd the pan; fry in batches, if necessary. Remove and drain on paper towels.

ROASTING

Roasting is often the preferred technique for cooking large pieces of tender beef, pork, lamb, or veal. Season the meat with a spice or herb rub and place it in a rack in a roasting pan just large enough to fit comfortably. Roast in a medium-high (350°F/180°C) to high (400°F/200°C) oven; cook larger roasts such as prime rib or pork loin at a lower temperature, and smaller, tender roasts such as pork tenderloin, rack of lamb, or beef fillet at higher temperature. This technique ensures even cooking and a tender, juicy roast with a browned, but not charred, exterior. You can also roast steaks and chops in a covered gas or charcoal grill using the indirect-heat method (page 106).

BROWNING STEAKS AND CHOPS

Initial searing and browning enhances the flavor of meat by sealing the surfaces and caramelizing the natural sugars in the meat to provide a rich, browned exterior. If you like, use a spice or herb rub to create a savory crust on the outside of the food when it is browned.

TESTING FOR DONENESS

The most reliable way to check for doneness when cooking meat or poultry is by using an instant-read meat thermometer. It should be inserted into the thickest part of a steak or chop—away from the bone, if there is one—to give you a quick read of the internal temperature. Always choose a thermometer that gives you actual temperatures (e.g., 125°F/52°C), and not just estimates such as "Rare beef."

Another way to test doneness is to cut into the meat near the bone for bone-in cuts and into the center of boneless cuts. If the interior meat is too pink for your liking, continue to cook. This technique, although certainly reliable, has the drawback of marring the presentation of the meat.

An old chef's trick is to prod the top of a steak or chop with your finger and then compare the tension in the meat to the muscle at the ball of your thumb. Make a fist with your thumb tucked in and touch the muscle. When the muscle is perfectly relaxed you have the equivalent of raw meat. Tighten the muscle slightly and you have the tension level of rare meat, tighter will be like medium rare, and tightest will equal well done. With a little practice, this works well, but keep a thermometer handy, just in case.

RESTING

Letting meat rest after removing it from the heat allows the juices to redistribute and the internal temperatures to equalize. This ensures juicy meat that is uniform in temperature. Tent the meat loosely with aluminum foil so that it won't lose too much heat. Meat will continue to cook slightly while resting, so it should be removed from the heat just before it reaches the desired doneness.

RECIPES

Here are some basic recipes that are used throughout the book, as well as popular side dishes that complement steaks and chops.

CHICKEN STOCK

4 fresh flat-leaf (Italian) parsley sprigs

1 fresh thyme sprig

1 bay leaf

6 lb (3 kg) chicken necks and backs

3 stalks celery

3 carrots, peeled and halved

2 yellow onions, halved

2 leeks, white and light green parts only, cleaned and sliced

Salt and freshly ground pepper

Wrap the parsley, thyme, and bay leaf in a piece of cheesecloth (muslin) and secure with kitchen string to make a bouquet garni.

Combine the bouquet garni, chicken parts, celery, carrots, onions, and leeks in a large stockpot. Add cold water to cover (about 3.5 qt/3.5 l). Bring to a boil over medium heat. Reduce the heat to low and let simmer, uncovered, for 3 hours, regularly skimming the foam from the surface. Taste and season with salt and pepper.

Strain the stock through a fine-mesh sieve into another container and discard the solids. Let cool. Cover and refrigerate until the fat solidifies. Discard the congealed fat. Pour into airtight containers and refrigerate for up to 3 days or freeze for up to 3 months.. Makes about 3 qt (3 l).

BEEF OR VEAL STOCK

4 lb (1.5 kg) beef or veal shank bones with some meat on them, cut into 3-inch (7.5-cm) lengths by the butcher

2 yellow onions, coarsely chopped

4 fresh flat-leaf (Italian) parsley sprigs

1 fresh thyme sprig

1 bay leaf

2 carrots, peeled and coarsely chopped

1 stalk celery, coarsely chopped

Preheat the oven to 425°F (220°C). Put the bones and onions in a lightly oiled roasting pan and roast until well browned, 35–40 minutes.

Wrap the parsley, thyme, and bay leaf in a piece of cheesecloth (muslin) and secure with kitchen string to make a bouquet garni.

In a large stockpot, combine the bones, onions, carrots, celery, bouquet garni, and 8 qt (8 l) water and bring to a boil over high heat. Reduce the heat to low and skim the foam from the top. Simmer, uncovered, for at least 3 hours or up to 6 hours, skimming occasionally.

Strain the stock through a fine-mesh sieve into another container and discard the solids. Let cool. Cover and refrigerate until the fat solidifies. Discard the congealed fat. Pour into airtight containers and refrigerate for up to 3 days or freeze for up to 3 months. Makes about 5 qt (5 l).

FRIED POLENTA

1½ cups (7½ oz/235 g) fine-ground polenta

Salt

2 teaspoons dried thyme

Freshly ground pepper

2 tablespoons vegetable oil

In a large saucepan over medium-high heat, bring 5 cups (40 fl oz/1.25 l) water to a boil. Whisking constantly, add the polenta in a slow, steady stream. Stir in 2 teaspoons salt, reduce the heat to medium-low, and continue to cook, stirring constantly, until the polenta thickens and pulls away from the sides of the pan, about 20 minutes. Spread the polenta to an even thickness on a rimmed baking sheet, cover with plastic wrap, and refrigerate until cool. Once cool, cut the cooked polenta into 1-inch (2.5-cm) by 2-inch (5 cm) slices. Sprinkle both sides with the thyme and salt and pepper to taste. Heat the oil in a heavy frying pan over medium-high heat until shimmering. Add the polenta slices and fry until browned, 3–5 minutes on each side. Makes 4–6 servings.

SCALLOPED POTATOES

2 lb (1 kg) russet potatoes, peeled and thinly sliced

2 teaspoons all-purpose (plain) flour

Salt and freshly ground pepper

2 tablespoons unsalted butter, at room temperature, cut into small pieces

2 cups (16 fl oz/500 ml) milk

1 tablespoon Dijon mustard

1 teaspoon Worcestershire sauce

Preheat the oven to 350°F (180°C). Grease a large roasting pan with 1 tablespoon oil. Arrange a layer of sliced potatoes in the bottom of the pan, sprinkle with flour, salt, and pepper and dot with pieces of butter. Repeat the layers until all the potatoes are used. In a small bowl, mix together the milk, mustard, and Worcestershire sauce and pour the liquid over the potatoes. Cover with aluminum foil and bake until the potatoes are tender, about 1 hour. Remove the foil and continue baking until the milk is fully absorbed and the top is browned, about 15–20 minutes longer. Makes 4–6 servings.

ROASTED POTATOES

2 lb (1 kg) small new potatoes

2 tablespoons olive oil, or more if needed

1½ teaspoons dried tarragon or thyme

1½ teaspoons paprika

1½ teaspoons garlic powder

½ teaspoon lemon pepper (page 98)

Salt

Preheat the oven to 400°F (200°C). Bring a large saucepan three-fourths full of lightly salted water to a boil. Add the potatoes and boil until they are not yet tender throughout but can just be pierced with the tip of a knife, 10–12 minutes. Drain, let cool, then toss with the olive oil, tarragon, paprika, garlic powder, lemon pepper, and salt to taste. Transfer to a roasting pan and roast, shaking the pan and turning the potatoes occasionally, until golden brown, about 20 minutes. Add more olive oil during roasting if the potatoes seem dry. Makes 4–6 servings.

SMASHED SWEET POTATOES

3 lb (1.5 kg) sweet potatoes, peeled and cut into 2-inch (5-cm) chunks

2 tablespoons unsalted butter

1 teaspoon salt

1 pinch *each* cayenne pepper and freshly grated nutmeg

Put the sweet potatoes in a saucepan with salted water to cover. Bring to a boil, reduce the heat to medium, and simmer until very tender, 15–20 minutes. Drain and return to the pan. Add the butter and salt. Smash the sweet potatoes until thoroughly broken up but not smooth. Top with a sprinkling of cayenne and nutmeg. Makes 6 servings.

SWEET POTATO BISCUITS

2 sweet potatoes, peeled and cut into 2-inch (5-cm) chunks

2 cups (10 oz/315 g) all-purpose (plain) flour

2½ teaspoons baking powder

½ teaspoon salt

½ teaspoon freshly grated nutmeg

¼ cup (2 oz/60 g) chilled unsalted butter, cut into chunks

Boil the potatoes in salted water and mash until smooth. Preheat the oven to 400°F (200°C). In a bowl, combine the flour, baking powder, salt, and nutmeg. Add the sweet potatoes and butter. Mix to break up the butter and incorporate the flour. Roll out the dough, cut the biscuits into rounds with an upside-down glass, and place them on an ungreased baking sheet. Bake until golden brown, 25–30 minutes. Makes 24 biscuits.

MINT PILAF

3 cups (24 fl oz/750 ml) homemade beef stock (page 110) or prepared broth

2 tablespoons olive oil

½ yellow onion, finely chopped

¼ cup (1½ oz/45 g) pine nuts

½ teaspoon *each* ground cinnamon and ground cumin

1½ cups (10 oz/315 g) long-grain rice

1 cup (1½ oz/45 g) chopped fresh mint

Salt and freshly ground pepper

In a saucepan, bring the stock to a boil over medium heat. Reduce the heat to medium-low and keep at a simmer. In another saucepan, heat the olive oil over medium high-heat. Add the onion, pine nuts, cinnamon, and cumin and sauté until the onion is translucent, about 5 minutes. Add the rice and sauté until coated with oil, 1–2 minutes. Add the stock and reduce the heat to low. Simmer, covered, until rice is tender, about 20 minutes. Remove from the heat, fluff the rice, and stir in the mint. Season to taste with salt and pepper. Makes 4 servings.

ROASTED GARLIC

2 heads garlic, tops cut off

2 tablespoons olive oil

Salt

Preheat the oven to 425°F (220°C). Place the garlic head in a roasting pan, drizzle with olive oil, and sprinkle with salt. Cover the pan with aluminum foil and roast until soft, about 45 minutes. Remove from the oven and let cool. Squeeze the garlic cloves out of their skins and mash with a fork.

GLOSSARY

ARBORIO RICE Arborio is an Italian rice with a large, plump grain and high starch content, which makes it ideal for risotto. Carnaroli is another good risotto rice, but it is a little harder to find in the United States. Both Arborio and Carnaroli are characterized as "superfine" rices.

ASIAN HOT SAUCE Asian chile oils and sauces come in many colors, flavors, and heat levels. Indonesian *sambal oelek* and *sambal badjak* are among the hottest. Chinese chile oil and sauce add both heat and flavor to marinades and stir-fries. Sriracha, a bright red, hot chile sauce from Thailand, delivers zest to many Southeast Asian dishes. Thai sweet chile sauce, a blend of sugar, water, and red chiles, is delicious on beef, seafood, and chicken. Look for these oils and sauces in well-stocked super-markets and Asian groceries.

CAPERS Caper bushes grow wild throughout southern France and around the Mediterranean. Before they can flower, the small, olive-green buds are harvested and preserved in salt or a vinegar brine. Pleasantly tangy, capers add a piquant bite to Provençal dishes. Salt-packed capers have a slightly more pungent bite and are worth seeking out. They should be rinsed and drained before using.

CHILES, HANDLING To reduce the heat of a chile, cut out the membranes or ribs, and discard the seeds. This is where the capsaicin—the compound that gives a chile its heat—is found. If you like heat, leave in a few seeds. Avoid touching your eyes, nose, and mouth while you are working with chiles. When finished, thoroughly wash your hands, the cutting board, and the knife with hot, soapy water. Wear kitchen gloves when working with especially hot chiles to prevent burns to your fingers.

COGNAC This double-distilled brandy is made only in the Charente and Charente-Maritime areas in western France. Smooth and potent, Cognac derives its distinctive flavors from the region's chalky soil in which the grapes are grown and from the special oak barrels used for aging. Cognac is labeled according to barreling age: V.S. (Very Special) has been aged for at least two years, while V.O. (Very Old), V.S.O.P. (Very Special Old Pale), and Réserve have been finished in wood for at least four years. Cognacs labeled X.O., Vieille Réserve, or Hors d'Age have been aged for at least six years, although many top-quality Cognacs are aged even longer.

CORNSTARCH Cornstarch, also known as cornflour, is used in many sauces for its thickening power. Just a spoonful can change a thin liquid into a thick and shiny sauce. The starch is first blended with a small amount of liquid, allowing smooth blending into a larger amount of liquid. After adding the cornstarch mixture, let the sauce simmer for a few minutes, both to thicken it and to remove the chalky taste of the starch.

GRILL BRUSH Designed for cleaning grills, this long-handled brush has rustproof bristles and a stainless-steel scraper. Use it while the grill is still hot after cooking to scrape off any food particles stuck to the rack.

HERBES DE PROVENCE Herbes de Provence is a fragrant, boldly flavored blend of dried herbs, usually including basil, thyme, oregano, savory, and laven-der. It may be purchased but is easy to make at home. The classic combination is 2 tablespoons dried thyme, 2 table-spoons *each* dried summer savory and dried basil, 1 teaspoon fennel seeds, and ½ teaspoon dried lavender.

HOISIN SAUCE This sweet, reddish-brown Chinese sauce is made from soy beans, sugar, garlic, five-spice powder or star anise, and a hint of chile. It can be thick and creamy or thin enough to pour. It is rubbed on meat and poultry before roasting, and also is used as a condiment. Hoisin sauce should be used judiciously, as its strong flavor can easily overpower most foods.

HORSERADISH Native to Europe and Asia, this gnarled root has a spicy flavor that perks up sauces and side dishes and pairs extremely well with roast beef and other cuts of meat. It can be found fresh but is more commonly sold bottled as "prepared" horseradish, already grated and mixed with vinegar or beet juice. The best prepared horseradish can be found in a market's refrigerated section.

LAMB CHOPS, FRENCHING To french lamb rib chops or racks, a butcher or cook cuts away and discards the fat, meat, and connective tissue between and around the tips of the bones, down to the meat. Rib steaks also can be frenched.

MADEIRA A fortified wine from the Portuguese island of the same name, Madeira is stored for at least three months in a warm room or tank, and sometimes aged further in wooden casks, where it develops a distinctive flavor reminiscent of burnt caramel. Madeira varies from the mellow and dry to sweet and robust. It is served as an aperitif, a dessert wine, or as a flavoring for rich sauces.

MARSALA Named for the Sicilian city in the area where it is made, Marsala is a fortified wine—that is, a wine preserved by the addition of brandy to raise the alcohol content. The rich-tasting, amber-colored wine is available in sweet and dry forms and is used in both savory and sweet dishes. Dry Marsala is enjoyed as

an aperitif; sweet Marsala is a welcome addition to pan sauces, and is also enjoyed as a dessert wine.

MASCARPONE This very soft, creamy, fresh Italian cheese is made from cow's milk. It has a texture reminiscent of sour cream but lacks its bite. Mascarpone is usually sold in plastic tubs.

MUSHROOMS Mushrooms absorb water readily and become soggy and flavorless if they are immersed for too long in water. To clean them, wipe with a damp cloth or brush. Following are some of the most popular varieties used in the recipes in this book:

Cremini: Also called common brown mushrooms, cremini are closely related to button or common white mushrooms. They have a firm texture and full flavor. Large, fully mature cremini are known as portobello mushrooms.

Oyster: Cream to pale gray in color, with a fan shape, oyster mushrooms have a subtle flavor similar to shellfish. They used to be found only as wild mushrooms but are now cultivated.

Porcino: Also called ceps, porcino mushrooms are pale brown and smooth and have a woodsy flavor. In the United States, porcini are most commonly available dried, although fresh mushrooms can be found in autumn.

Shiitake: Meaty in flavor, these Asian mushrooms have flat, dark brown caps

usually 2–3 inches (5–7.5 cm) wide and a rich, almost tealike flavor. They are available fresh or dried.

White: These cultivated, all-purpose mushroom are sometimes referred to as button mushrooms, although this term refers specifically to young, tender white mushrooms with closed caps.

MUSTARD POWDER Mustard seeds come in three colors: white (also called yellow), brown, and black. The white seeds are the mildest, followed in pungency by brown and black. English mustard powder is the preferred form of mustard powder and is a classic blend of ground white and brown seeds with some added wheat flour.

NUTS, TOASTING Toasting nuts gives them a crisp texture and attractive golden color. To toast nuts in the oven, spread them in a single layer on a baking sheet and bake them in a 350°F (180°C) oven for 10–12 minutes, turning once to brown all sides. To toast them on the stove top, place them in a dry, preferably cast-iron, frying pan and cook them, stirring frequently, until golden, about 5 minutes; keep a close eye on the nuts, as they can burn quickly; make sure to remove them from the pan as soon as they are browned.

ONION, SWEET Some regions have become known for growing sweet, mild onions that are excellent for cooking and eating raw. These include Maui from

Hawaii, Walla Walla from Washington, and Vidalia from Georgia. You'll find them in the produce section of well-stocked supermarkets.

PINEAPPLE, PEELING To peel a pineapple, first cut off the crown with leaves and the bottom. Set the pineapple straight up on one end and cut off the skin in long vertical strips with a paring knife. Cut off the brown "eyes" by laying the pineapple down and cutting a shallow furrow along the diagonal of the eyes; then scoop them out with the tip of your knife. Core the pineapple using an apple corer or a thin, sharp knife, and slice as desired.

PORK MEDALLIONS Medallions are easy-to-prepare cuts from the tenderloin, the boneless, almost fatless piece of meat that runs down a pig's back. Medallions are perfect for quick grilling or sautéing.

POTATOES, NEW Harvested in spring and early summer, new potatoes are usually quite small and of the round red or round white variety. They are low in starch and will keep their shape well after cooking. Be aware that not all small red and white potatoes are new. A true new potato is freshly harvested, will have a thin skin, and will not keep long.

SHALLOTS These small members of the onion family have delicate lavender-veined lobes under papery gold skins. Milder than onions, shallots turn sweet and mellow when cooked, and they are used in many recipes where the harsher flavor of onion would be overpowering.

SILVER SKIN On some cuts of meat you'll find a thin membrane called silver skin. It is completely innocuous, but if it is not removed, it will cause steaks to curl during cooking.

STAR ANISE Distinctively shaped star anise is the seed-bearing pod from a Chinese evergreen tree. Slightly more bitter than aniseed, star anise is used in Asian cuisine to flavor teas and savory dishes. In the West it is often used in baked goods.

TARRAGON VINEGAR Tarragon vinegar is simply white vinegar that has been flavored with tarragon. You can find it in most well-stocked supermarkets.

TEQUILA Tequila is made from the steamed, fermented, and distilled juice of the blue agave (a close relative of the century plant). There are three styles: sharp-tasting *blanco*, also known as silver or white tequila, is aged in steel for sixty days; *reposado* is aged in wooden casks for sixty days; and the more refined *añejo* spends at least one year in wooden casks.

TOMATOES, ROASTING Whole fresh tomatoes can be rubbed with olive oil and seasoned with herbs, garlic, and olives or just salt and pepper and roasted in the oven to heighten their flavor and cook them slightly. You can serve them whole, halved, or quartered as a garnish, or you can chop them to make a light and easy tomato sauce with minced garlic and more herbs. Roasting tomatoes on the grill is easy. Leave them uncored and cook over indirect heat in a covered grill, or follow the directions for oven-roasting (page 24).

WORCESTERSHIRE SAUCE A traditional English condiment, Worcestershire sauce is an intensely flavorful and savory blend of varied ingredients, including molasses, soy sauce, garlic, onion, and anchovies. Popular in marinades for grilled food, it can also be passed at the table.

ZINFANDEL Although long considered a California native, the Zinfandel grape in fact has the same DNA as Italian *primitivo*, which originated in Croatia. The varietal was brought to California in the late nineteenth century, somehow acquiring the name Zinfandel along the way. This full-bodied red wine gives off an aroma of blackberries and spice, and its substantial structure and robust flavor make it a great complement to hearty foods like grilled or broiled steaks and chops.

INDEX

SIMON & SCHUSTER SOURCE
A division of Simon & Schuster, Inc.
Rockefeller Center
1230 Avenue of the Americas
New York, NY 10020

WILLIAMS-SONOMA
Founder and Vice-Chairman: Chuck Williams

WELDON OWEN INC.
Chief Executive Officer: John Owen
President and Chief Operating Officer: Terry Newell
Vice President, International Sales: Stuart Laurence
Creative Director: Gaye Allen
Series Editor: Sarah Putman Clegg
Editor: Emily Miller
Designer: Leon Yu
Design Assistant: Marisa Kwek
Production Director: Chris Hemesath
Color Manager: Teri Bell
Shipping and Production Coordinator: Todd Rechner

Weldon Owen wishes to thank the following people for their generous assistance and support in producing this book: Copy Editor Carrie Bradley; Contributing Editor Dan Warrick; Food and Prop Stylists Kim Konecny and Erin Quon; Photographer's Assistant Faiza Ali; Proofreaders Desne Ahlers and Arin Hailey; and Indexer Ken DellaPenta.

Set in Trajan, Utopia, and Vectora.

Williams-Sonoma Collection *Steak & Chop* was conceived and produced by Weldon Owen Inc., 814 Montgomery Street, San Francisco, California 94133, in collaboration with Williams-Sonoma, 3250 Van Ness Avenue, San Francisco, California 94109.

For information regarding special discounts for bulk purchases, please contact Simon & Schuster Special Sales at 1-800-456-6798 or business@simonandschuster.com

Color separations by Bright Arts Graphics Singapore (Pte.) Ltd.
Printed and bound in Singapore by Tien Wah Press (Pte.) Ltd.

First printed in 2004.

10 9 8 7 6 5 4 3

Library of Congress Cataloging-in-Publication data is available.

ISBN 0-7432-6186-0

A NOTE ON WEIGHTS AND MEASURES

All recipes include customary U.S. and metric measurements. Metric conversions are based on a standard developed for these books and have been rounded off. Actual weights may vary.